Double Counterpoint

AND CANON.

DOUBLE COUNTERPOINT

AND CANON.

BY

EBENEZER PROUT, B.A. Lond.

(Professor of Harmony and Composition at the Royal Academy of Music),
Author of "Harmony: Its Theory and Practice,"
"Counterpoint: Strict and Free," etc.

SECOND EDITION.

HASKELL HOUSE PUBLISHERS Ltd.
Publishers of Scarce Scholarly Books
NEW YORK. N. Y. 10012
1969

First Published **1893**

HASKELL HOUSE PUBLISHERS L<small>TD.</small>
Publishers of Scarce Scholarly Books
280 LAFAYETTE STREET
NEW YORK, N. Y. 10012

Library of Congress Catalog Card Number: **68-25300**

Standard Book Number 8383-0312-9

Printed in the United States of America

PREFACE.

VARIOUS causes have conduced to the somewhat long delay in the appearance of the present work. Since the second volume of this series (*Counterpoint, Strict and Free*) was issued, the author, at the request of the publishers, has compiled four small books supplementary to *Harmony* and *Counterpoint*. This for some time prevented his commencing the present volume. But the chief cause of the delay has been the difficulty of the task itself. A book which, like the present, deals with many of the most abstruse problems of musical theory, required a great deal of preliminary work, not only in examining and comparing existing treatises, but in writing a very large number of examples to illustrate the various points touched upon. Such a book, if produced in a hurry, would be of little or no value. The author is by no means unaware of its shortcomings ; but he can at least honestly claim for it that he has spared neither time nor trouble in its preparation, and that he has done his best to make it practical and useful, especially for those who are studying without the aid of a master.

As mentioned in the preface to *Counterpoint*, it was originally intended to include the subject of Fugue in this volume. To have done so, however, would have necessitated the omission of so much which it is desirable that the student should know, and would have compelled the author to treat of Fugue itself in such a cursory, not to say perfunctory manner, that he soon decided to confine the present volume to Double Counterpoint and Canon, and to deal with Fugue in a separate work, which shall follow this as soon as he can find time to write it.

In treating of double counterpoint, it has been thought advisable to begin with it, as with simple counterpoint, in the strict style. It must, of course, be borne in mind that this is merely preliminary technical work to such double counterpoint as is used in actual composition It has been necessary in some respects to relax the strictness of the rules when applying them to double counterpoint—especially in the tenth, the most difficult interval to work. The fundamental principles of strict counterpoint are, nevertheless, observed; and the author believes that writing under restrictions will be of great value to the student, as giving him freedom in the later stages of his work. The whole of the examples to the strict double counterpoint have been written expressly for this work.

In treating of free double counterpoint, the plan pursued in the preceding volumes of this series, of taking the examples, as far as possible, from the works of the great masters, has been adhered to. It will be seen that the quotations are both more numerous and longer than in *Counterpoint*. This is because the student now approaches more nearly to actual composition, which can be better learned from the study of good models than in any other way. It is impossible to teach the invention of melody, though the general principles of its forms may be made intelligible enough; but the exercise of the imagination may be stimulated by the study and analysis of existing masterpieces; and though it is not to be expected that the student will ever acquire the skill of a Bach, yet, from the examination of that composer's works, he can at least discover many general principles to guide him in his own efforts. The chapters on double counterpoint on a florid subject, and with free parts, largely consist of analyzed extracts from the works of the great composers.

The subject of double counterpoint in the rarer intervals is passed over in silence by most theorists. Though far inferior in importance to those more frequently employed, these double counterpoints are not without interest; and, as they are more often used than is generally supposed, a chapter is given to this subject, in which some curious examples will be seen. In the last chapter of the first part of the book, an attempt has been made to simplify the difficult study of triple and quadruple counterpoint.

The second half of this volume, which deals with Canon, presented more difficulties to the author than the first, chiefly because of the impossibility of giving on many points any beyond the most general directions. In one respect, it is believed, the present book differs from most of its predecessors. A great part of the instructions on canon to be found in many treatises has reference to matters which are not of the slightest practical use to the student. It is doubtful whether it is worth while for any-body at the present day to trouble himself about writing an infinite canon by augmentation, a *canon cancrizans*, or a riddle-canon. Yet the old text-books give elaborate instructions for the composition of these musical puzzles, for they are nothing better. As the object of these volumes is to teach what the student may really need, these subjects are not dealt with at all, though, for the sake of completeness, specimens of all the varieties are given. Only such canons are treated of in detail as possess true musical value, and the learner who masters these will find that he knows all that is really necessary for him. The study of double counterpoint, and of the various forms or imitation is an invaluable and indispensable introduction to the higher branches of composition, and amply rewards the musician for the somewhat severe labour necessary for its acquirement.

The author has to acknowledge his obligations for assistance from several quarters. He is indebted to a series of articles by Mr. J. S. Shedlock, in the *Magazine of Music*, for calling his attention to some of the examples of counterpoint in the rarer intervals in Bach's "Wohltemperirtes Clavier." He has to thank Mr. F. Corder for the canon in § 453, and Herr E. W. Fritzsch, of Leipzig, for permission to reprint the canons in §§ 452, 468 from the *Musikalisches Wochenblatt*. His warm thanks are again due to Dr. C. W. Pearce, not only for valuable suggestions, but for his kindness in revising the proof-sheets of the volume—a more than usually troublesome work, owing to the large amount of music type.

LONDON, *July*, 1891.

TABLE OF CONTENTS.

PART II.—CANON.

augmentation, 299—By diminution, inverted and direct, 300—Close imitation by contrary motion, 301—By inversion in a major key, 302—"Per arsin et thesin"; partial imitation, 303—Double imitation by inversion, 304—Canonic imitation in four parts, 305—Directions for the practice of imitation, 306—The use of imitation in actual composition, 307.

DOUBLE COUNTERPOINT
AND CANON.

—◆—

PART I.—DOUBLE COUNTERPOINT.

CHAPTER I.

INTRODUCTION.

1. Before commencing the study of the present volume, the student will be presumed to have completed his course of Harmony and of simple Counterpoint, both in the strict and free styles. He will therefore be fully aware that by the word Counterpoint in its general sense is meant the art of combining two or more independent melodies so as to make correct harmony.

2. If two melodies which are to be played or sung together are so written as to be capable of inversion, that is, if either of them may be above or below the other, and the harmony still be correct, we have *Double Counterpoint*, a term which simply means "invertible counterpoint." The word "double" is appropriate, because each of the two parts has a double function; it may serve either as an upper melody, or as a bass. If three or four melodies are combined, any one of which can be a highest, lowest, or middle part, we have triple or quadruple counterpoint, according to the number of voices. We shall deal first with Double Counterpoint, reserving Triple and Quadruple for a later part of this volume.

3. The first thing necessary for the student in commencing this branch of work is to enlarge his conception of the meaning of the term *Inversion*. Hitherto the word has always been used in one sense—that of changing the relative position of notes by putting one of them one or more octaves higher or lower than before, or sometimes by placing one note an octave higher and another an octave lower. Thus, when we speak of a sixth as being the inversion of a third, we mean that one of the two notes of the interval is placed an octave higher or lower than before. Similarly, the inversion of a chord means the changing the relative position of some note or notes of that chord, one of them being the root, thus altering its pitch by one or more octaves. But in

B

double counterpoint the inversion may be at *any* interval, though inversion in the octave is the most common, and the most useful.

4. It is important that the student should be able to calculate with ease and accuracy what intervals are produced by the inversion of other intervals at any given distance, and also, when two counterpoints are inverted with respect to one another, at what interval the inversion is made. He already knows (*Harmony*, § 26*) that the number of the inversion of an interval in the octave is found by subtracting the number of the interval itself from 9. The reason we subtract from 9 and not from 8 is, of course, because the note of the interval which does not change its position is reckoned twice. Thus a sixth is the inversion of a third; and $3+6=9$. We do not usually make inversions at a less interval than an octave, because if either melody were of any considerable compass, it is probable that some of the notes would cross, and there would be no inversion. If, for instance, we write two subjects,

and then try to invert them in the fifth, either by placing the lower part a fifth higher or the upper part a fifth lower, it is evident that the parts will cross, and that at the ✳ there will be no inversion, the part which was the higher still remaining so.

For this reason inversions at a less distance than the octave are not used; but any distance beyond the octave may be taken.

5. It is a general rule that two subjects which are to be inverted must not be at a greater distance from one another than the interval of their inversion. In the example just given there was no inversion in the fifth at ✳ because the two notes were originally more than a fifth apart. But it would have been quite possible to invert the passage in the octave,

or in the tenth,

because these intervals are nowhere exceeded in the distance between the two parts. The practical objection to inversion at a

---

* The references to "*Harmony*" and "*Counterpoint*" throughout this volume are in all cases to the author's books on those subjects. (Augener & Co.)

less distance than the octave is, that it restricts the range of the melodies too much.

6. We saw just now that the inversion of an interval in the octave was found by subtracting the number of the interval from 9, and we gave the reason for this. The same reason applies to inversion at any other distance. Hence we get a simple rule of universal application :

To find the inversion of an interval at any distance, subtract the number of the interval itself from the next number above that of the distance at which it is to be inverted.

7. An example or two will make this perfectly clear. We wish to know what a fifth becomes when inverted in the tenth. The next number above 10 is 11, and $11-5=6$. The pupil can verify this at once. In the first example in § 4 the last crotchet of the first bar is the fifth above G. In the inversion in the tenth in § 5, the D has become B, the sixth below G. Similarly, to find the inversion in the twelfth, subtract from 13 ; in the fourteenth, subtract from 15, and so on in every case. It ought to be added that the only intervals commonly used for inverting are the octave or fifteenth (the double octave)—the latter being necessary if the two melodies are more than an octave apart— the tenth, and the twelfth. Inversions at the other intervals are very rare ; we shall give a few examples later in the volume.

8. In analyzing compositions containing double counterpoint, such as fugues, it is often useful to be able to ascertain the interval in which two subjects have been inverted. The process here is exactly the converse of that in the preceding case. Observe the two intervals in their different positions ; add their numbers together, subtract 1 from the total, and we get the interval of inversion. For instance, if we find that a third by inversion has become a sixth, $3+6=9$. Take 1 from 9, and we see that the inversion was in the octave. If the third by inversion had become an octave, $3+8=11$, the interval of inversion was the tenth ; if it had become a tenth, $3+10=13$, and the inversion was in the twelfth.

9. It sometimes happens, in double counterpoint other than the octave, that the two voices will be in the same *relative* position to one another, but the counterpoint will be at a different interval, as in the following passages from Bach's Fugue in B flat (No. 45 of the "Wohltemperirtes Clavier")—

Here the themes are the same in both passages, but the intervals are different. To find the nature of the counterpoint in such a case, invert the *smaller* of the two intervals *in the octave*, add the other interval to the inversion, subtract 1, and the remainder gives the interval of inversion. In the above example, if we take the third quaver of the first bar, we see a tenth at (*a*), an octave at (*b*). Of these, the octave being the smaller, we invert it; it becomes a unison; 1 + 10 = 11; therefore the double counterpoint is in the tenth. If we take the first note of the second bar, we obtain the same result. The third at (*b*) being the smaller of the two intervals, we take its inversion, the sixth, and add it to the fifth at (*a*), 6 + 5 = 11; and here again the rule we have just given holds good.

10. We shall now give an example of double counterpoint in all the usual intervals, taken from No. 40 of Bach's Forty-Eight Fugues in the "Wohltemperirtes Clavier," which will illustrate the rules we have given. We shall not quote the full harmony where it is in three or four parts, but shall merely extract those voices which are in double counterpoint with one another. At the 5th bar of the fugue we find the following passage—

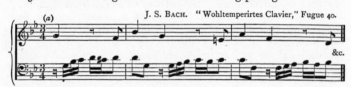

J. S. Bach. "Wohltemperirtes Clavier," Fugue 40.

At the 13th bar we see it inverted thus—

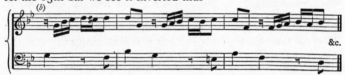

To find the interval of inversion, we take any of the notes in both passages, and add their intervals. Let us take the first note in the second bar. At (*a*) the interval is a sixth, at (*b*) it is a tenth, 6 + 10 = 16; the inversion is therefore at the fifteenth or double octave. We know that in harmony a tenth and a third are practically the same interval. If we call the interval at (*b*) a third, we get 6 + 3 = 9, therefore double counterpoint in the octave, which is virtually identical with that in the fifteenth.

11. Later in the same fugue, we meet with some different inversions. At the 28th bar is the following—

(The alteration of the first note of the lower part here is the result of the construction of the fugue, and has nothing to do with the double counterpoint.)   It will be seen that the rest is identical with the upper part of (*a*).   Here we notice that the lower part of (*a*) is transposed a twelfth higher, and we have double counterpoint in the twelfth.   Let us apply our test, as before, to the first interval in the second bar.   At (*a*) it was a sixth, it is now a seventh, and $6 + 7 = 13$.   Lastly, at bar 36, we get another inversion—

Here the upper part is almost the same as at (*c*), but the bass is a sixth lower.   To be certain of the distance of the inversion here, we must once more apply our rule.   The first interval in the second bar at (*a*) was a sixth; its inversion is a fifth.   As $6 + 5 = 11$, the double counterpoint here is in the tenth.   If the student has understood these examples, he will have little difficulty in analyzing any combination he may meet with in the works of the great masters.

12. In treating Double Counterpoint we shall begin, as with simple counterpoint, by working it in the strict style.   It must be understood that this is simply the preparatory technical work to the free Double Counterpoint used in actual composition.   To those who have conscientiously worked at strict counterpoint, it will present but little difficulty.   We take first double counterpoint in the octave and fifteenth, as being the most used and the most useful.

CHAPTER II.

STRICT DOUBLE COUNTERPOINT IN THE OCTAVE AND FIFTEENTH.

13. We have incidentally said in the last chapter (§ 9) that double counterpoint in the octave and in the fifteenth were virtually identical. The only practical difference between the two is, that in the former the two parts may not be more than an octave apart, and in the latter they may. But with this exception, all the rules for the one apply equally to the other ; and, in fact, double counterpoint in the fifteenth is, far more often than not, spoken of as being in the octave.

14. It is evident that inversion in the octave changes neither the names of the notes of the inverted part nor the intervals between the successive notes of the melody, the only alteration being that of pitch. We shall see later that this is not the case in any other species of double counterpoint. But while the names of the notes of the inverted part remain the same, its relation to the part with which it is inverted is entirely different. This will be clearly seen by placing under one another in two columns all the intervals up to the octave with their inversions.

INTERVALS: 1 2 3 4 5 6 7 8

INVERSIONS: 8 7 6 5 4 3 2 1

Notice that, as mentioned in the last chapter (§ 4), the number of the interval added to that of its inversion amounts to 9 in every case.

15. On examining the above table, we shall see that the dissonant intervals (the second and seventh) are also dissonant in their inversions, while perfect and imperfect consonances also do not change their nature by inversion in the octave. But, as we are now writing in two parts, the lower part must always make a correct bass to the upper one (*Counterpoint*, § 113). The perfect fifth when inverted, becomes a perfect fourth ; and, in the strict style which we are now studying, a fourth with the bass is always a dissonance (*Counterpoint*, § 29). The perfect fifth, therefore, although a consonance, can only be employed in strict double counterpoint in the octave under special limitations, which we shall explain as we proceed.

16. It will further be noticed that an octave when inverted becomes a unison. Though the octave may be used freely in simple counterpoint, the unison is only allowed on the first and

last notes of an exercise. A little more liberty may be permitted
in this respect in double counterpoint; it will nevertheless be
well for the student to avoid the octave and unison as far as
possible on an *accented* note, excepting at the beginning or end of
a counterpoint, though their employment is not absolutely prohibited. If the double counterpoint is in the fifteenth, this
caution, as regards the octave, need not be attended to, as the
octave below then becomes the octave above, and *vice versa.*

17. In double counterpoint in the fifteenth, it will often be
found convenient, instead of changing the position of one voice
by two octaves, to place one part an octave higher, and the other
an octave lower than before ; in many cases, indeed, this may be
necessary in order to keep the parts within a reasonable compass
Take for example the following passage—

As these two subjects are in two places more than an octave
apart, it is clear that they must be inverted in the double octave.
But if we place the upper part two octaves lower, the first note
of the second bar will be ≡≡, which is too low ; and if we
transpose the bass two octaves higher, the last note will be ≡≡·
It will therefore be best to put the upper part an octave lower,
and at the same time the lower part an octave higher, thus—

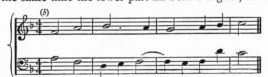

It will be seen that the *relative* position of the two parts to one
another is precisely the same as if one had remained stationary,
and the other had been transposed two octaves, but that both are
now in a convenient position.

18. We will now proceed to double counterpoint of the first
species. The chief point to notice here is, that it is impossible
to use the interval of the fifth at all, because by inversion it
becomes a fourth, which in strict two-part writing is unallowable.
Care must also be taken not to exceed the compass of the octave
between the two voices, unless the inversion is in the fifteenth.
If the subject leaps much, it will often be impossible to avoid the
overlapping of parts (*Counterpoint*, § 31); this is less objection-

able in double than in simple counterpoint.   The only available
form of cadence in this species is

19. One point remains to be mentioned.   Owing to the
necessity of retaining the same melody above and below the
subject, we can allow ourselves rather more liberty than in simple
counterpoint as to *implied* harmony.   This refers more particularly to the interval of the third above the mediant, which in the
majority of cases will represent I*b*, and not III*a*.   The inversion
of this interval can only represent III*b*, and many cases will
occur in which this chord has to be followed by one of those
which, in the "Table of Root Progressions" (*Counterpoint*, p. 32),
is marked as only "possible."   We may be content now if we
avoid the absolutely *bad* progressions.

20. The best way of writing exercises in Double Counterpoint
is to use a score of three staves, placing the Canto Fermo in the
middle, and writing the counterpoint above, and its inversion
below.   It will, of course, be understood that no three-part
harmony is implied ; but this method gives the best opportunity
of observing the two melodies in their dual relation to one
another.   It will be well to indicate this by a double brace at
the beginning of the lines, thus—

21. We will now take two of the subjects so often treated in
Counterpoint, and work on them double counterpoints of all
species, beginning with the first.   We take first a subject in a
major key—

It will generally be found convenient to write the counterpoint and its inversion (when in the octave) for two voices, the compass of which is an octave apart ; either (as here) the subject in the alto with the counterpoints in treble and tenor, or (as in some of the examples we shall presently give) the subject in the tenor with the counterpoints in alto and bass. The two basses—the subject when the counterpoint is above, and the counterpoint when the subject is above—should always be figured. The only point requiring notice in the example just given is that in the third and fourth bars of the inversion the parts overlap (§ 18). The only way to have avoided this would have been to take the unison A as the fourth note of the upper part, and this would have been far more undesirable than the course we have adopted. The repetition of the note C would have been extremely weak ; no repetition of a note should be allowed in two-part counterpoint.

22. In our next example we will, for the sake of variety, write the counterpoint in the 15th.

We here write the inversion in the bass, as it would be too low for a comfortable tenor part. Notice at (*a*) the chord III*b*, and observe its progression. The third interval (*b*) is marked as a chord of the sixth. The tenth (or third) $_E^G$ might also represent III*a* ; but if we so consider it here, the progression to the following chord (III*a* to IV*b*) is one of the bad ones, while if we regard it as I*b*, the progression from III*b* to I*b*, though not one of the strongest, is at least possible. Here is an illustration of what was said in § 19.

23. Now let us look at the inversion of this counterpoint. At the third bar we find III*b* again. The following chord (*c*) may equally well represent IV*a* and II*b* ; but (as at (*b*) just noticed), we regard it as II*b* here, because III*b* to II*b* is a good progression, while III*b* to IV*a* is only a possible one. At (*d*) we see another of the weaker progressions, III*b* to V*b*. These will often be necessary in strict double counterpoint of two parts.

24. We will now take a subject in a minor key. As with simple counterpoint, this will be found more troublesome than a double counterpoint in the major, because of our smaller choice of harmony. We therefore, as usual in cases of difficulty, permit ourselves a little more liberty. The octave and unison may be

somewhat more freely used than in a major key. But the most
important concession refers to the harmonizing the mediant of
the scale. In simple counterpoint the sixth below the mediant
is forbidden (*Counterpoint*, § 118), because of its implying a chord
which is unavailable. But if we disallow it here, we shall be
also prevented from using the third above the mediant, representing I*b*; and the only possible notes to place above the
mediant will be the octave or unison and the sixth. It will often
happen that neither of these will be good ; therefore, as the sixth
below the mediant is itself a consonance we can use it, if necessary, in *double* counterpoint, though it implies no available chord,
because here the claims of melody are superior to those of
harmony. In figuring this interval it will be well to put the 6 in
brackets, thus—(6)—to show that it implies an *interval* only,
and not a chord. An illustration of this point will be seen in the
example now to be given—

25. Here we have intentionally taken a subject which is not
very easy to work. Let it be noticed that the upper melody is
here almost, so to speak, compulsory. We can take no other
note than the octave to commence with ; as the lower counterpoint should not begin with a first inversion. The fourth note
of the subject is the only one which allows a choice of harmony,
and if instead of D (representing II*b*), we take the chord of IV*a*,
every note of that chord gets us into trouble. F in the upper
part gives either a unison or bad hidden octaves ; C would be a
repetition of the preceding note ; if we take the upper A, we have
a seventh with one intermediate note ; while the lower A must
either be followed by the unison, or by a leap of an augmented
interval. Up to the fifth bar, therefore (to borrow a metaphor
from the chess-board), every move is virtually forced.

26. Now look at (*a*), bar 6. The E flat of the subject can
only bear a first inversion above it ; the only possible notes of
the counterpoint are C, E, and G, the root, third, and fifth of
the tonic chord. Our cadence is already fixed (§ 18) ; if we
take C here, we shall not only have the very weak repetition
, but the whole counterpoint will consist,
with the exception of the fourth note, of nothing but C and B♮.

E flat will not do here; we cannot come down by similar motion to
a unison, to say nothing of the impossible leap of an augmented
fifth; and if we take the upper octave we break a law of melodic
progression (*Counterpoint*, § 19), for after the leap of a diminished
fourth we do not return within the interval. We have therefore
absolutely no good note here but G, and we consequently take it
in spite of the fact that its inversion will represent an interval, and
not a chord. It will not often be needful to use this interval in
any other than the first, and sometimes the fourth species, because
of the larger resources at our disposal. Observe that it would
have been possible to take G also at the third bar of this example;
we did not do it then, because there was no necessity for it.

27. For the sake of getting more variety in the melody, we
will make our next counterpoint at the 15th.

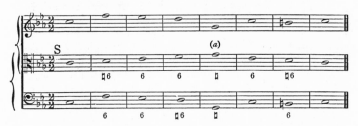

After the full explanation given of the last example, but few
remarks are needed for this. At (*a*) we have taken the unison
as the best note available; B♮ would have led to the same position as in the last example; we cannot repeat the D; and if we
take E (the interval of the sixth which we have just been discussing), we shall have four consecutive sixths between the two
parts. Though these are not so strictly prohibited in double as
in simple counterpoint, it is well to avoid them if possible.
Besides this, we wished to show that a counterpoint could be
written on this subject without using the sixth above the dominant
at all.

28. In double counterpoint in the octave, of the second
species, the dissonant intervals (the seconds, fourths, and
sevenths) can be introduced as passing notes on the unaccented,
and even occasionally on the accented, parts of the bar. The
fifth, being the inversion of the fourth, can also be thus used;
but it is important to remember that it can only be taken in an
upper part in a descending, and in a lower part in an ascending,
passage. A moment's thought will show the student the reason
for this.

29. The cadence of the second species differs in an important
respect from that of any other. It is impossible in this species

to make a cadence which can be properly inverted. The usual
cadences for simple counterpoint in the upper part are

If we invert (*a*) in the octave, we shall have a fourth below the
subject on the accented beat; while (*b*) will not invert in the
octave at all; and though possible to invert it in the 15th, it
would still not be good to do so, because of the weak progression
of the harmony with inversions of two chords in the bar. On
the other hand, of the usual cadences in the lower voice

(*b*) exceeds the limit of an octave, and all three when inverted
give a fourth taken as a harmony note, instead of as a passing
note. For this species, therefore, the cadence is always free, that
is to say, no attempt is made to invert it, but the last three or
four notes of the two counterpoints are quite different. It should
be noted that the forms (*b*) of both upper and lower cadences
are available for double counterpoint in the octave, though containing the interval of a tenth, as they have not to be inverted.

30. We now give some examples of the second species, taking
the same subjects as before—

At (*a*) we see the fifth introduced on the second beat of the bar
as a passing note. The last four notes in the inversion show the
free cadence spoken of in the last paragraph. As with simple
counterpoint of the second species, it is best to take passing
notes, where practicable, on the unaccented beats, in order to
secure a smoother melody.

31. We now write another double counterpoint, also in the
octave, on the same subject, endeavouring to get as much variety
as possible.

At (*a*) and (*c*) will be seen the unison on the unaccented beat. At (*b*) is the perfect fifth used as an auxiliary note, and not (as in the last example) as a passing note.* At (*d*) we have an auxiliary note quitted by leap of a third (*Counterpoint*, § 165). This device should be sparingly used in strict writing; it is introduced here to obtain a better melody. The only other notes available would have been A, which would have been weak here (compare the preceding and following bars), or F, which would have given in the next bar a seventh with one intermediate note.

32. We next take our minor subject, and first write to it a double counterpoint in the octave—

The only point to notice here is that the inversion of the third bar at (*a*) gives the interval of the sixth above the dominant (§ 24). Here, however, we distinctly have a chord implied in the second half of the bar, viz.: I*b*. We have, therefore, figured the interval with (6) and exceptionally marked the implied harmony under the second minim of the bar.

33. One more example of the second species will suffice, and this shall be in the fifteenth.

* For the distinction between auxiliary and passing notes see "*Harmony*," § 255.

At (*a*) the bass evidently implies two chords in the bar. Though we rejected this progression for the cadence, it may occasionally be introduced in the course of a counterpoint. Special attention should be given to (*b*). Here the sixth above the dominant at the beginning of the bar does not of necessity imply the bare interval, as in the third bar of the last example. On the contrary, it is better here to regard it as an accented passing note ; and the passage shows us the one exceptional case in which the fifth may be taken as a harmony note. It must be on the second half of the bar, preceded by an accented passing note, and (as its inversion will be a fourth) it must be, as here, quitted as well as approached by step. It is but seldom that opportunity will occur for its use ; it is introduced here to show under what circumstances it is possible.

34. In the third species the general rules for simple counterpoint of the same species are mostly to be observed. A fifth can still only be taken as a passing or auxiliary note ; the exceptional treatment of this interval shown in our last example is seldom practicable with four notes to one. But the rule which restricts the employment of the fifth of a chord in the lowest part (*Counterpoint*, § 223) is considerably relaxed in double counterpoint, as its use in an upper part would otherwise be extremely limited. It may in double counterpoint be taken on any part of the bar except the first ; it is, however, better not to use it below the root when this note is present, unless the fifth is so treated as to have something of the character of a passing note, or come between other notes of the chord. Illustrations of these points will be seen in our next example.

35. Excepting on the first beat of the bar, an octave in this species should never be approached by conjunct motion, as its inversion will give the unadvisable progression from a second to a unison. This, though *possible* when the second is a passing note, should be avoided altogether in strict double counterpoint. The only good cadence for this species is, with four notes to one,

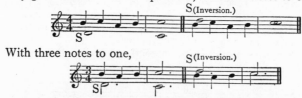

With three notes to one,

36. Our first example of this species with four notes to one

shows at (*a*) how little variety is sometimes possible in commencing one of these counterpoints. When the subject leaps, as here, from tonic to dominant, there is no other good commencement than that given here, or in the following example, which it will be seen is almost identical. A double counterpoint is mostly harder to write on a subject that leaps than on one that moves chiefly by conjunct degrees. At (*b*) in the inversion is seen the fifth of the chord below the root. Notice that here the root is not present, and we do not trouble ourselves, as in simple counterpoint, about the *implied* $\frac{6}{4}$. At (*c*) the root is present, but here the G, coming between F and A, though a note of the chord, acquires the character of a passing note.

37. In our next example, written on the same subject,

it will be seen that except the cadence no bar is the same as in the last counterpoint. At (*a*) the fifth is taken below the root, but (as at (*b*) of the last example) the root is not present in the upper part. At (*b*) the A in the bass is figured as a sixth, because the implied harmony (VII*b* to I*a*) is good, while II*a* to I*a* would be bad.

38. We next give two examples of four notes against one in a minor key—

After the explanations already given, the only remarks to be made on these counterpoints are, that at (*a*) in the inversion of the first example two chords in the bar must be implied; and that, as with the examples in the major, every bar in the two exercises is different, except at the cadence, for which there is no other good form.

39. Counterpoint with three or six notes to one being so much less frequently used than that with four, it will suffice to give one example of each.

These counterpoints require no explanation.

40. The fourth species is very difficult to work in strict double counterpoint, owing to the limited means at our disposal. The suspensions 9 8 and 4 3, with their inversions are available; but 6 5 is evidently inadmissible, as also is 7 8 in an upper part, though its first inversion 5 6 can be taken. We are also greatly restricted as to our syncopations by the prohibition of the fifth. The only good cadence for this species is

If the suspension cannot be prepared, the cadence must be free, as in the second species.

C

41. It would be easy to write subjects against which it would be absolutely impossible to put a double counterpoint strictly of the fourth species. The student therefore, though it will be well for him to work a few exercises of this kind, need not devote much time to it; the fifth will repay him much better for his labour. We give two examples, as specimens—

It so happens that this subject can be very easily worked; it has not been needful to break the syncopation at all.* Note that at (*a*) the unison is taken, because otherwise we should have had five consecutive sixths between subject and counterpoint. Let the student also mark at (*b*) the fifth as a prepared suspension in the *lower* voice, and ask himself why it could not be equally so taken in an upper part.

42. Our minor subject is much more difficult to treat satisfactorily.

Observe that at (*a*) we are forced to break the suspension, as the G, if tied, would in the bass have become a fourth below the subject. At (*b*) it is only possible to continue the suspension by taking the rather unsatisfactory interval of the sixth above the dominant. Notice also that the inversion of (*a*) must evidently imply two chords in the bar.

---

* The author has, since writing this counterpoint, discovered that it is identical with the example he had given in § 268 of *Counterpoint*. The coincidence is purely accidental; the earlier book was not referred to at all while writing these exercises.

43. The fifth species will be found not only less difficult, but
more interesting to work than the fourth. The best forms of
cadence are

The student will by this time be quite able to see the inversions
for himself. The form of cadence at (*a*) is on the whole best;
but (*b*) will be needful if it be impossible to prepare the suspension, as, for example, if the subject ends ⟨music⟩.

It should also be noticed that it will now be possible to take the
fifth of a chord as a harmony note in the upper voice, though this
could not be done in the fourth species. Our next example will
show how this is to be managed.

44. We now give some specimens of the fifth species—

At (*a*) we have the fifth of a chord taken as a harmony note in
the upper voice. As it becomes a fourth by inversion, it must
of course be prepared, and it must descend; the fourth, to which
it descends, becomes a fifth in the inversion. It will be seen that
those notes which in the upper counterpoint are harmony notes,
become passing notes in the lower, and *vice versa*. At (*b*) of the
lower counterpoint we have the implied bad chord progression
II*a* to I*a*. We have more than once said that in double counterpoint, considerations of root progression, though not to be wholly
disregarded, are of less importance than a good flow of melody.

45. For the sake of getting more melodic variety, we will write our next example in the fifteenth, instead of the octave—

At (*a*) in the upper counterpoint, there are no consecutive octaves with the subject, because the tied E at the beginning of the bar is a note of the harmony. The lower counterpoint at (*b*) must clearly imply two chords in the bar.

46. We now give two examples of the fifth species in a minor key—

Very little explanation is needed here. At (*a*) of the first
example, we see the same treatment of the fifth as a consonance
which was noticed in § 44. At the first bar of the second
example at (*a*) it looks as if the suspension were prepared by a
crotchet. Though this would not be absolutely forbidden, it is
best in general that the preparation should be a minim. In the
present case the G has been already sounded as the first note of
the counterpoint, and the mental effect is therefore quite satisfactory. In the two examples just given, an effort has been
made to obtain as much variety as possible, both in melody and
rhythm.

47. It is comparatively seldom that in actual composition we
find double counterpoint written against a subject, the notes of
which (as in the *canti fermi* given in this chapter) are of equal
length. Here are two examples, as specimens—

Far more commonly both the parts which are in double counterpoint are in notes of unequal length—two parts of the fifth

species, so to speak. This kind will be dealt with later, when we come to treat of free double counterpoint.

48. We conclude this chapter by giving a few subjects for double counterpoint in the octave. It will hardly be possible to write ten or twelve different exercises on the same *canto fermo*, as with simple counterpoint; to do this well, would require the mastery of resource of a Bach. But with patience and perseverance, the student will generally be able to invent two or three counterpoints in each species, except the fourth. When he has worked all the subjects given here, he may take any of those to be found in any treatise on counterpoint, or, if he prefers, he may write *canti fermi* for himself. As soon as he has acquired fluency in strict double counterpoint, he will be ready to commence the far more interesting study of the free double counterpoint of Bach, Handel, and the great masters who have followed them.

SUBJECTS FOR DOUBLE COUNTERPOINT IN THE OCTAVE.

CHAPTER III.

STRICT DOUBLE COUNTERPOINT IN THE TENTH.

49. Double Counterpoint in the Tenth is that in which a counterpoint to a given subject is inverted a tenth higher or lower, as the case may be. But, as the interval of a tenth consists of an octave and a third added together, there are two other ways of inversion in the tenth. One of the two parts may be raised an octave, and the other lowered a third; or one may be lowered an octave and the other raised a third. It is important that the student should clearly grasp the fact that, whichever of these four methods of inversion be chosen, the *relative* position of the two notes to one another will remain the same, though their absolute pitch will be different in each case.

50. An example will make this perfectly clear.

At (*a*) is the interval of the perfect fifth. Let us invert it in the tenth in the various ways just described. If we keep the upper note in its place, and put the lower note a tenth higher, we have (*b*); if, on the other hand, we put the upper note a tenth down, we get (*c*). Now move both, but in opposite directions, just as we did in § 17 when inverting in the fifteenth. If we raise the lower part a third, instead of a tenth, and bring the upper part down an octave, we have (*d*), which it will be seen is the same as (*b*), but an octave lower; and lastly, if we lower the upper part a third, and raise the lower part an octave, we get (*e*), which is the same as (*c*) an octave higher. The important point to notice is that in each case the inversion of the fifth gives the same interval—the sixth, though in two cases it is a major, and in two a minor, sixth.

51. The above example shows one of the chief differences between double counterpoint in the tenth, and that in the octave. When a note of any interval is inverted in the octave, its name always remains the same; but inversion in the tenth always

changes the name of a note.   To find the inversion of any
interval in the tenth, we subtract the number of that interval
from 11 (§ 6).   This gives the following table—

INTERVAL :   1   2   3   4   5   6   7   8   9   10
INVERSION IN THE TENTH :   10   9   8   7   6   5   4   3   2   1

Of course no interval larger than a tenth can be used in this
counterpoint (§ 5).

52. It will be seen from this table that every consonance
when inverted in the tenth remains a consonance, and every dissonance remains a dissonance.   It will further be noticed that
the perfect consonances (the unisons, fifths, and octaves) become
imperfect consonances (tenths, sixths, and thirds) when inverted,
and *vice versâ*.   The perfect fourth is of course a dissonance in
two-part counterpoint.   The only exceptions to the general rule
given above are that the sixths above the subdominant, both in
the major and minor key, and above the submediant and leading
note in the minor key, become dissonant fifths by inversion.
This point we shall notice later.

53. It must be further remarked here that inversion in the
tenth changes not only the names of the notes but their position
in the scale, and their consequent relation to one another.   For
example, if we take the first three notes of the scale of C, and
invert them either in the tenth above or in the tenth below, we
change the position of the semitones—

At (*a*) we see a tone between the first and second notes, and
another tone between the second and third.   If we invert the
passage a tenth higher, as at (*b*), we have a semitone between the
first and second, and a tone between the second and third notes ;
while the inversion a tenth lower, as at (*c*), gives a tone between
the first two notes, and a semitone between the second and third.
It will thus be seen that the whole character of a melody is
changed by inversion in the tenth, unless we add accidentals to
take it into another key.

54. If we now turn to the table of inversions given in § 51,
we shall be able to draw some inferences which will assist us in
making rules for writing double counterpoint in the tenth.   In
the first place, we notice that as the third by inversion becomes
an octave, and the sixth becomes a fifth, it is impossible to have
consecutive thirds or sixths, such as we are accustomed to in
simple counterpoint, or in double counterpoint in the octave.
Hence we get our first general rule :

No consecutive intervals of any kind are allowable.

55. Now we go one step further.   We know that in strict

counterpoint hidden fifths and octaves are altogether forbidden. But if, in double counterpoint in the tenth, we approach either a third or a sixth by similar motion, the inversion of the passage must give an octave or a fifth also approached by similar motion. Therefore, in this counterpoint we cannot employ similar motion at all, and our second rule is :

Only contrary and oblique motion are available.

As no repetition of a note is allowed in the first species, we are in this evidently restricted to contrary motion.

56. The limitations to which we have to submit in writing double counterpoint in the tenth are by no means exhausted yet. There are various intervals, both in harmony and melody, which we shall now see are unavailable, because they cannot be inverted without breaking rules. If the subject contains the subdominant, this note cannot have a sixth above it, because its inversion in the tenth below will give the interval of the diminished fifth. The leading note in the subject can in a major key take no interval but a sixth above it; because the third when inverted would give a doubled leading note, while the fifth is a diminished fifth, and the octave is obviously impossible. In a *minor* key, there is no note that can be placed above the leading note—at all events in the first species; because here the inversion of the sixth gives the augmented fifth. In other species the difficulty may be evaded in some cases by treating the augmented fifth as an accented auxiliary note.

57. There are also several pitfalls to be avoided in the melodic progressions. The leap in an upper part from the supertonic down to the submediant, and its converse, the upward leap from submediant to supertonic, give in the tenth below the interval of the tritone.

Tenth below.

If the counterpoint is in the lower part, it is clear that the leap up from supertonic to dominant, and its converse, will also give a tritone when inverted in the tenth above.

58. In the minor key we are even more hampered, in consequence of the four augmented intervals to be found between various degrees of the scale. The simplest way to show the intervals to be avoided will be by the table here given—

Unavailable in upper part.　(a)　(b)　(c)　(d)

Augmented Intervals.

Unavailable in lower part.

The middle staff shows the four augmented intervals of the minor key. The upper staff shows the intervals which if inverted in the tenth below will give augmented intervals, and the lower staff shows intervals which become augmented when inverted in the tenth above. We have omitted the lower intervals at (*b*) and the upper ones at (*c*) because there is no danger with these, as they are tritones themselves, and the student will of course avoid them. Some of these intervals, however, can be occasionally saved, as will be shown later, by the use of the melodic forms of the minor scale.

59. It will be seen that double counterpoint in the tenth requires so much to be avoided that its rules may be compared to the laws of the Decalogue, nearly all of which begin with the words, "THOU SHALT NOT." Consequently, this kind of counterpoint is far less frequently met with, and much less useful than that in the octave. It is nevertheless important that the student should be able to work it, and he will find its practice very beneficial. But, as he will have to work under such difficulties, he need not now trouble himself at all about implied root-progressions, and may content himself if his melodies are good.

60. It is not every subject which is suitable for double counterpoint in the tenth, especially in the strict style. In actual composition, where we are free to make our own parts, we should, of course, take care to write the two melodies with special reference to their inversion in the tenth ; but with many of the ordinary *canti fermi* it will be found all but impossible to write a satisfactory counterpoint of this kind. To illustrate this, we will take the major subject which we used in the last chapter, for double counterpoint in the octave, and try to write a double counterpoint in the tenth on it. We give the subject, numbering the notes, for convenience of reference—

We shall take the first species, as being the simplest, and also because the harmonic progressions will almost always be the same in the other species. We shall not have the same freedom of choice here that we should have were our double counterpoint in the octave.

61. As our exercise should begin with the tonic chord in root position, our first note above the C of the subject must be E ; for the octave C, if inverted in the tenth, would give A in the bass, while G would give E, representing the first inversion. We must, of course, take E as the *tenth* above C—not the third, or the parts will cross on the next note. Of course if the second note of the subject is below the first, we must begin with the

third, or else the contrary motion with the second note will make
us exceed the allowed interval of the tenth.

62. For our second note we have not much choice. We
already know that we must move in contrary motion to the subject (§ 55). If the upper part falls to B, the inversion will give
octaves by contrary motion. The unison, though sometimes
necessary, should not be used if it can be avoided. Here D is
obviously the best note, giving B as its inversion. If for the
third note we rise to G, its inversion gives the unison; we therefore return to E.

63. Thus far we have had no difficulty at all; but now our
troubles begin. The best note to put above 4 will clearly be C;
but then what shall we do with 5? As this note is the subdominant of the key, we cannot have D above it (§ 56), nor can
we rise to A, because the inversion will give octaves by contrary
motion. The only possibility is F, the octave of the subject.

64. The subject (5, 6) now falls from F to E; our counterpoint must therefore rise to G—the only possible note (§ 51).
But from E the subject again falls to D; and the counterpoint
must either exceed the limit of a tenth, or move in similar

motion, both of which are forbidden.   We are therefore in a fix, and must "try back."

65. We will now for our fourth note take the unison A instead of C.   This will alleviate our sufferings somewhat, but not much. The student will see that we can now take C for our fifth note, and E for the sixth ; we can even go up to F for the seventh—

We are obviously no better off than we were before.   But we have a loophole for escape.   In double counterpoint in the tenth, as with the second species in the octave, the cadence may, if necessary, be free, *i.e.*, the last two bars need not be invertible. Sometimes it is possible to continue the inversion to the very end ; sometimes only the last note need be free.   In the exercise we have been working the best close would have been this—

Here the lower counterpoint at 6 7 moves in thirds with the subject; but this does not matter, as the second third is not intended for inversion.

66. We have entered in some detail into the difficulties incidental to this kind of counterpoint, so that the student may know what points are to be more particularly attended to in working his exercises.   We said above that subjects for double counterpoint in the tenth should be specially adapted for that purpose.   Instead, therefore, of treating the same subjects as in the last chapter, we shall write two, one in a major and one in a minor key, and work them in each of the five species.   For our major subject we choose the following—

It will be noticed that we have avoided all large intervals.   A

subject which leaps much will often be found somewhat troublesome for treatment in the tenth.

67. A double counterpoint of the first species against this
subject gives very little difficulty.

The only points to notice in this example are that at (a) we see
in the upper counterpoint the false relation of the tritone, which
we disregard here (though we would not allow it in double
counterpoint in the octave), because we do not trouble ourselves
about root-progressions provided our melodies are good; and
that, except the last note of the bass, at (b), the inversion is kept
up throughout. It would have been possible here to keep the
inversion to the very end by writing the last half of the counterpoint thus—

In our next example we shall see the close strict.

68. We now take a subject in the minor—

Observe that at (a) we use in the lower voice the *melodic* form of
the minor scale. This is often advisable; in the present case the
G of the subject takes the fifth in the upper counterpoint; if we
write the third, B, we must either make it B♮, as we have done
below, or have an augmented second from B♭ to C♯, which we
must obviously avoid. Moreover, the use of the B♮ here allows
us to continue the strict double counterpoint to the last note.

69. In the second species of double counterpoint in the
tenth, we shall evidently have oblique motion on the unaccented
half of each note of the subject. It is best, where possible, still

to approach the accented notes by contrary motion, though occasionally, in other species than the first, similar motion may be
employed, *provided that the progression between the two accented
notes is contrary.* (See below the examples to §§ 76, 77.) It is
often possible to continue the double counterpoint strictly to the
very end ; but this need not be insisted on, and a free cadence
will often produce a better effect, as in the example to § 71 below.

70. In the following example of this species

will be seen at (*a*) a passing note quitted by leap of a third
(*Counterpoint*, § 165), and the same procedure is repeated in
the next bar. This is done to obtain a better melody. In the
third bar we cannot take the upper G instead of E, or we shall
have a seventh with one intermediate note ; and, apart from the
similar motion, we cannot have either B, or the lower G—the
former because its inversion gives consecutive octaves, and the
latter because of the leap of a tritone to the following C♯. At
(*b*) we give two forms of cadence ; that in small notes preserves
the double counterpoint to the end ; but because of the leap of
the leading note, it is musically less commendable than the free
cadence given in large notes. The inversion of this latter
(marked in small notes in the tenor part) would not be so
advisable as a cadence, and the last note must still be free, as
we obviously cannot finish on the submediant.

71. Our minor counterpoint of the second species

shows at (*a*) an effective employment of an accented passing
note. In this species, these may be used without hesitation if
the melody is improved thereby. In this example, the strict
close is even less good than in the major given above. A free
close here is decidedly preferable.

72. We now take the same subjects for the third species—

At (*a*) we have apparently implied the commencement of the lower counterpoint with a first inversion. But if the student will try for himself, he will see that the only other possible commencements here were in the upper part,

The two leaps of an octave at (*a*) are certainly not desirable; neither would the sixth preceded by a third in the same direction, as at (*b*), be good. We have, therefore, preferred to begin as above, which gives both the third and fifth of the chord in the upper part, and neutralizes, as far as possible, the effect of the third in the bass by putting the root of the chord both before and after it. The final note of the bass is, of course, free.

73. It will be seen that in commencing our counterpoint on the minor subject

we can use a passing note at the end of the bar, which was

impracticable with the other *canto fermo.* The only point requiring remark in this example is the bar of counterpoint at (*a*).
The fourth note, F♯, in the upper part must either imply a false
relation with the harmony, or a major chord on the subdominant.
Its inversion in the bass cannot be satisfactorily explained, from
a *harmonic* point of view, according to the laws of strict counterpoint. The progression is here, nevertheless, perfectly good, and
it is introduced to impress upon the student's mind that in this
difficult branch of his art he need not trouble himself at all
about the *implied* root-progressions, if only his melodies and the
counterpoint in itself are correct. It must be remembered that,
in actual composition, double counterpoint in the tenth is only
written in the *free* style. Even in this there are restrictions
enough in all conscience; and if in addition we hamper ourselves by limitations very useful in simple counterpoint, but quite
needless here, we shall lade ourselves with burdens grievous to
be borne, and good writing will become almost impossible.

74. The force of what has just been said will be seen when
we attempt this counterpoint in the fourth species. Here it is
absolutely necessary that the rules for simple counterpoint of
this species must be to some extent relaxed; because, as similar
motion is not permitted, whenever the subject descends, the
suspension must ascend. The student will remember that the
only ascending suspension allowed in simple counterpoint is that
of the tonic by the leading note; but when inverted in the tenth,
above or below, we shall no longer have the suspension of the
same degree of the scale. We therefore so far modify the rule
as to allow the use of all rising suspensions (just as in harmony),
provided they move by step to a consonance. The fourth species
then becomes tolerably easy to work.

75. In our first example of this species

we are able, with the liberty we are now allowing ourselves, to
avoid breaking the syncopation at all. At (*a*) is the upward
suspension 5 6, while at (*b*) the suspension of the tonic by the
leading note has become by inversion that of the submediant by
the dominant. At (*c*) we make the close free for the same reason
as in § 70.

76. In our example in the minor,

the progression at (*a*) must be specially noticed. It has been needful here to break the syncopation, because if we held the D from the last bar, it could not be followed by E (§ 56); neither could we rise to G, because the inversion would give a tritone (§ 58). If we fall from D to B, we must break the suspension here, or we shall have an augmented second; and the third bar from the end is a much better place than the last but one for breaking the syncopation. It will be seen also that the suspension 7 6 in the upper part gives as its inversion 4 5; that is, the fifth is approached by similar motion. This would have been wrong had the B of the tenor been the only harmony note of the fifth bar; but here G is also a harmony note, and we therefore have contrary motion from accent to accent (§ 69).

77. The fifth species is by no means the most difficult to work in the tenth.

We need only say of this example that at (*a*) is a precisely similar instance in the lower part to that explained in our last counterpoint, and that the small notes at the end of the upper part show, as with some of the preceding examples, the possibility of continuing the counterpoint strict to the end.

D

78. Our last example

requires no explanation.   The progression to the cadence is the
same as in the two examples last given.   To keep strictly to
contrary motion here, we must either have had an augmented
second or a major third above the subdominant.

79. It was said in § 49 that inversion in the tenth could be
effected in various ways.   The student will see that in all the
examples given we have never changed the position of the *canto
fermo* by placing it a tenth higher or lower.   This is because
if we did so, we should so alter its character as to render it
unsuitable for our purpose ; for it would not then end on the
tonic, and we should either have to finish with an inversion of
the tonic chord, were the transposition of the subject upwards,
or with the submediant chord if we transposed downwards.   In
writing exercises on a *canto fermo*, the student should follow the
same plan.   We may again remind him that these exercises are
nothing more than the technical preliminaries for actual composition ; in free writing, as we shall see later, the other methods of
transposition can also be employed.   We probably never find
double counterpoint in the tenth used throughout a piece ;
and when it is met with, it is mostly accompanied by free parts
(that is, parts not in double counterpoint), filling up the harmony.
None the less will working in the strict method prescribed in this
chapter be of great value to the student.

80. A peculiarity of this variety of counterpoint, in which it
differs from all other kinds,* is that the upper and lower counterpoints can be employed simultaneously against the subject,
excepting, of course, where the close is free.   They will be evidently in tenths (or sometimes in thirds or sixths, by transposing
one of them an octave), throughout.   Examples of this will be
seen when we come to speak of free double counterpoint.

81. We have already said that it is not all subjects which are
adapted for double counterpoint in the tenth.   We therefore give
a few *canti fermi* written specially for the purpose.   The student
should work on each subject one counterpoint in each of the
five species.   It will be difficult to invent more than one, as his

* Excepting the very rarely used double counterpoint in the thirteenth (see
Chapter VIII.).

resources are so limited, but it will not be necessary in any case to break the strict rules obligatory upon him, and working at these unquestionably troublesome exercises will go far to lighten his subsequent labours.

SUBJECTS FOR DOUBLE COUNTERPOINT IN THE TENTH.

N.B.—From this point the close must be free.

CHAPTER IV.

STRICT DOUBLE COUNTERPOINT IN THE TWELFTH.

82. Double counterpoint in the twelfth, as its name implies, is that which is designed for inversion in the twelfth above or below. As the twelfth is the octave of the fifth, it is evident that we can also invert two parts at this interval by transposing one of them an octave, and the other *in the opposite direction* in the fifth, just as in double counterpoint in the tenth we can transpose one part an octave and the other a third (§ 49).

83. The double counterpoint we have now to consider is far more used, and far more useful, than that in the tenth. It is also so much easier to work that the student who has laboured through the last chapter will, on arriving at this one, experience something of the same feeling of relief as a mountaineer, who, after toiling up a terribly steep and rough place, comes to a piece of comparatively level ground. He must not, however, expect to find double counterpoint in the twelfth, especially in the strict style, quite so easy as that in the octave.'

84. A moment's thought will show us that inversion in the twelfth (or fifth) changes the character of a melody far less than that in the tenth; for, with one exception, the semitones will remain in the same place in the scale. Thus, if we transpose the scale of C a fifth upwards, we shall have the scale of G without an F♯; while if we transpose it a fifth downwards, we get the scale of F without a B♭.

85. We will now make our table of inversions in the twelfth, as we did with the octave and tenth—

INTERVALS :   1   2   3   4   5   6   7   8   9   10   11   12
INVERSION IN THE 12TH : 12 11 10 9. 8   7   6   5   4   3   2   1

This table shows us that octaves become fifths, and fifths octaves, while thirds become tenths, and tenths thirds. This latter fact will obviously facilitate our work greatly, since we shall be no longer prohibited (as in double counterpoint in the tenth) from the use of consecutive thirds, or of similar motion. The interval requiring special care is the sixth, which, as by inversion it becomes a seventh, can in the strict style only be used as a passing note, or as a prepared discord. We shall give an example presently (§ 100) of its employment in this way.

86. As by transposition in the twelfth the position in the scale of every note is altered, we shall find, as we did with the

tenth in the last chapter, certain harmonic combinations and
melodic progressions which it will be needful to avoid, because
their inversion will produce prohibited intervals.   For harmonic
reasons, we cannot take an octave above the subdominant in either
the major or minor key, because the inversion of the upper note
a twelfth will give us the diminished fifth above the leading note.
Neither, for a similar reason, can we in a minor key take the
octave above the submediant, or the octave below the supertonic
or mediant.   The melodic progressions to be avoided will be best
shown by a table similar to that which we made for double counterpoint in the tenth (§ 58).

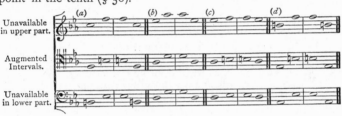

We have given the progressions in the key of C minor, to show
all the augmented intervals; but the student must observe that
those given at (*a*)—from tonic up to subdominant, and its converse, in the upper part; and from leading note up to mediant,
and its converse, in the lower part—are also unavailable in a
major key, as the tritone between subdominant and leading note
exists in that key also.

87. In writing double counterpoint in the twelfth it will be
best for the student to use the treble and bass voices for the
counterpoint and its inversion, and to put the subject in either
the alto or tenor—it is immaterial which.   He must, of course,
be careful not to exceed the compass of a twelfth between
subject and counterpoint.

88. An important point to notice in this kind of counterpoint
is, that the cadence must always be free.   The reason for this
will be evident with a moment's thought.   A subject for strict
counterpoint always ends on the tonic, and generally has the
supertonic as the penultimate note.   Let us take these two notes,
and try to write either above or below them a cadence which will
invert in the twelfth—

The cadence at (*a*), which is that usually employed in simple counterpoint and in double counterpoint in the octave, is clearly out of the question here, not only because the sixth by inversion becomes a seventh, but because if the upper counterpoint ends on the tonic (whatever precedes it) its inversion must end on the subdominant. To end the upper counterpoint on the mediant, as at (*b*), is no better; for the inversion will end on the sub-mediant. If, on the other hand, we write a good cadence in the bass, and attempt to invert it, we get a cadence which is simply atrocious in the treble, as at (*c*). In two-part writing, the student will remember, a third should not be followed by a fifth when both parts move by step, except in going from submediant to dominant (*Counterpoint*, § 157). The counterpoint against the last two notes of the subject will therefore always be free.

89. As double counterpoint in the twelfth is so much easier than that in the tenth, it will not be needful to write special subjects for working it, as we did in the last chapter. We shall, for the sake of comparison, take the same two subjects which in Chapter II. we employed for double counterpoint in the octave, and will give one major and one minor example in each of the five species.

90. As every exercise should commence with the tonic chord, unless the subject begins with the dominant, it is evident that our upper counterpoint should always have the fifth (or twelfth) of the subject for its first note ; otherwise the inversion will begin on the subdominant or submediant. If the subject should happen to begin with the dominant, we can put either the fifth or octave above it ; in the former case the lower counterpoint will commence with the dominant, and in the latter with the tonic.

91. We will now give double counterpoints of the first species—

These counterpoints are so intelligible that we need only direct the student's attention to the free close at (*a*) in each, of which we spoke just now.

92. Counterpoint of the second species is mostly not very difficult in the twelfth. As with the octave and tenth, passing and auxiliary notes may be introduced, occasionally even on an accented beat, as in the following example—

At (*a*) we have taken a seventh as an accented passing note in the upper part, which allows us to use a sixth as a harmony note in the bass. Let the student compare the introduction of the fifth as a harmony note in double counterpoint of the octave in the examples, §§ 44, 46. It is necessary to begin to make our cadence free at (*b*) in the third bar from the end. If the student will try, he will find no second note for this bar which can be properly inverted.

93. We next take our minor subject—

At (*a*) we have made on the unaccented notes of the second and third bars consecutive octaves with the subject. These should mostly be avoided, but here it was important to have A as the second minim of the third bar, and there was no other good note but G for the second minim of the second bar. The only way to avoid the octaves here would have been to introduce a transient modulation, by taking E flat as the first note of the third bar thus—

This would have saved the effect of octaves (see *Counterpoint*, § 175), but as a modulation would have been unadvisable, we have preferred to allow ourselves a small license here. In the inversion there is no effect of consecutive fifths, because of the decided mental impression of two chords in the third bar. We were anxious to keep A in the third bar, so as to be able to introduce the sixth as a harmony note in the following bar in such a manner as that its inversion shall be an accented passing note—see (*b*). Here we have the converse of the progression at (*a*) in our last example, where the passing seventh was in the upper part, and the sixth in the lower. At (*c*), as at (*b*), of § 92 we have to begin to make our cadence free.

94. Our next example (third species)

requires few remarks. At (*a*) two chords in the bar are clearly implied. Had we begun as we shall in the next counterpoint,

we should have consecutive fifths, and in the inversion consecutive octaves, by contrary motion. We need never hesitate about taking two chords in a bar, if we find it advisable. At (*b*) we are able to use the sixth again as a harmony note, because we can take its inversion in the bass as a passing seventh.

95. The only points to be noticed in our next example

are that at (*a*) the descending form of the minor scale with the
major sixth is used because the leading note is a harmony note;
that at (*b*) we have the same treatment of the sixth as in the last
example; and that at (*c*) we can equally well use the major and
minor sixth and seventh of the scale.

96. The fourth species is mostly very troublesome in double
counterpoint in the twelfth, because we are unable to employ one
of the most useful of all the suspensions—viz., 7 6, as its inversion will evidently give 6 7 in the bass. The difficulties of this
species will be illustrated in the examples we shall now give—

Until the counterpoint becomes free, at ✳ it is impossible to
obtain any conjunct motion against this subject, as the student
will soon find if he tries it. At ✳ it is best to break the syncopation. We have given an alternative version; but this is distinctly
less good, first, because we have four consecutive thirds between
the subject and the upper counterpoint, and secondly, because
we end on the third of the key instead of the tonic, and our
cadence contains no leading note.

97. Against our minor subject the counterpoint will be rather
more flowing, but not much better.

Our progression for the first three bars is forced, but the effect
of the fourth in the bass going to the fifth, at (*a*), can certainly

not be called satisfactory, though there is really nothing else to
be done here.   It will be seen that at the beginning of the fourth
bar it is absolutely necessary to break the syncopation.   The leap
of the octave at (*b*) is virtually compulsory.   In the fourth
species the syncopation should never be broken for two consecutive bars (*Counterpoint*, § 263); if we take B for the second note,
we get the unavailable suspension 7 6, besides a tritone in the
inversion (§ 86); if we take the only other possible note, D, the
inversion of the 9 8 suspension gives the 4 5 in the bass, which
we were forced to take in the third bar, but which should be
avoided wherever possible.   At (*c*) we have again broken the
suspension in the upper part, to avoid the weak close,

98. Taken altogether, the fourth species of double counterpoint in the twelfth is so unmanageable (to say nothing of its
being of hardly any practical use), that the student is not recom
mended to spend much time over it.   It is given here for the
sake of completeness, and a few exercises may be worked on it as
a preparation for the fifth species ; but there its utility ends.

99. Lastly we take our two subjects for counterpoint of the
fifth species—

It will be seen that this example is far more satisfactory, from a
musical point of view, than those of the fourth species.   At (*a*)
we have apparently consecutive octaves in the upper part and
consecutive fifths in the lower, with the first note (which is here a
harmony note) of the second bar.   Observe the way in which

they are saved by interposing two other notes of the harmony, both of which are *beyond* the first note of the third bar, so as to return by contrary motion. Such a procedure is often used in simple counterpoint to save *hidden* octaves and fifths (*Counterpoint*, § 178); we extend the principle here, so as to save actual consecutives. We must, however, add that it would have been bad to do this had not the first note in the second bar been a *tied* note, held on from the preceding chord, so that the note on the second crotchet has the character of the real harmony note of the bar. We have to begin our free cadence at (*b*), in the third bar from the end, as in the second and fourth species.

100. For our next example we transpose our subject to G minor, so as to keep our counterpoints in a better compass.

In this example we have illustrated at (*a*) the use of the sixth as a harmony note. It should be, as here, prepared *in the bass*; it must then continue to descend by step to the harmony note of the next chord. By comparing the upper and lower counterpoints in this bar, it will be seen that the harmony notes of the one become passing notes of the other, and *vice versâ*. We have already met with something similar in the examples in §§ 44, 46, 92, and 93. At (*b*) we have used a sixth again in the upper part, as we did in the counterpoints of the third species (§§ 94, 95). This enables us to continue the inversion to the end of the bar, by using the form of cadence shown at (*c*). Had we taken the same cadence as in the last example, we must have broken the inversion in the middle of the third bar from the end.

101. The student may now proceed to work double counterpoint of the twelfth in the different species on any of the subjects

given at the end of Chapters II. and III., or on any of those contained in *Counterpoint*. When he has acquired a mastery of this kind of writing, he may congratulate himself that his labours in the domain of *strict* counterpoint are at an end. He will find double counterpoint in the free style comparatively easy, if he have prepared himself for it by a conscientious course of hard work at the preliminary and technical part. The fundamental principles to be borne in mind will be the same by which he has hitherto been guided, and with which he may reasonably be supposed to be now familiar; but the strict study he has been through will give him a command of free writing, without fear of his abusing his liberty, which, it may be confidently affirmed, can be obtained in no other way.

CHAPTER V.

FREE DOUBLE COUNTERPOINT IN THE OCTAVE, TENTH AND TWELFTH, ON A CHORAL.

102. In writing double counterpoint, at whatever interval, in the free style, the student will have at his command (as with simple free counterpoint) all the resources of harmony. Chromatic chords may be introduced or implied; auxiliary notes may be taken by leap; in fact, all the additional freedom which was allowed in Chapters XIII. and XIV. of *Counterpoint* may be taken advantage of now. There is, however, one important difference to be borne in mind. All the exercises in simple counterpoint in the free style were in four parts. For the present our double counterpoint will be in two parts only; and for this reason, as the lower part has always to be considered as the bass, we must avoid the interval of a bare fourth between the two voices, unless it is used as a prepared suspension or a passing note. When we come, in a subsequent chapter, to treat of double counterpoint with added parts, we shall find it possible to employ the fourth more freely.

103. As the work on which we are now about to enter is in reality a species of actual composition, we are no longer restricted as to the length of our notes. It is therefore unnecessary to practise writing in any other than the fifth species; and in this we allow ourselves in one respect greater liberty than heretofore. In strict counterpoint it is rarely good, with the fifth species, to have two or more consecutive bars of the same pattern (*Counterpoint*, § 310). But we may now employ the same figure— especially sequentially—for several bars, if desirable, provided that the treatment does not become monotonous. It is no uncommon thing in the works of the great masters to find a double counterpoint constructed almost entirely on one pattern.

104. An important modification of our previous rules, and one that will greatly facilitate our work is, that in free double counterpoint dissonant notes may be sounded together, not only when (as in the strict style) one of them is an accented passing or auxiliary note, but also *when the two taken together clearly represent a fundamental discord.* Numberless illustrations of this might be given from the words of Bach; a couple will suffice here, both taken from his " Fifteen Inventions in two parts "—a work which contains some admirable examples of double counter-point in two parts only.

105. In the first of these Inventions the opening bars are subsequently inverted thus—

At (*a*) in the first bar an augmented fourth is sounded between the two parts, implying a third inversion of the dominant seventh. In the seventh bar the passage is inverted in the octave (or more strictly speaking, in the fifteenth), and at (*c*) the augmented fourth becomes a diminished fifth, which implies the first inversion of the dominant seventh. The first note of bar 8 is free, that is, it is not an inversion of the corresponding note of bar 2 ; but the second half of this bar is an inversion of bar 2 *in the twelfth.* The student will see this at once, by comparing the intervals at (*b*) and (*d*). The fifth at (*b*) becomes an octave at (*d*) ; 5 + 8 = 13 ; the inversion is therefore in the twelfth (§ 8).

106. Now look at the dissonant notes in this passage. Against the second quaver of (*b*) a seventh (an accented passing note) is struck in the bass ; this by inversion becomes a sixth—a harmony note (compare the progression at (*b*) in our example to § 93). The semiquavers C and A against the third quaver of (*b*) represent with the F above a chord of the sixth ; in the inversion at (*d*) the fourth becomes a ninth, and the sixth becomes a seventh against the bass note, which is itself the auxiliary note here, the implied harmonic progression being

This example shows how possible it now becomes to use many progressions hitherto forbidden.

107. Our next illustration is taken from the same work—

Bars 13, 14.

Here the inversion is in the fifteenth throughout; but, as this is virtually the same as the octave, we shall in future adopt the more usual name, and speak of such double counterpoint as being in the octave, unless there is any special reason for describing it otherwise. This example illustrates three different uses of dissonant notes. The seventh at (*a*) is a 7 6 suspension, inverting at (*d*) as 2 3; at (*b*) the dissonant fifth is a harmony note, and we have the first inversion of a dominant ninth; the augmented fourth at (*e*) gives the third inversion of the same chord; at (*c*) and (*f*) we see accented passing notes. The examples at (*b*) and (*e*) are those bearing more immediately on the point we are now discussing. Let it be also noticed that the passage just given exemplifies what was said at the end of § 103, the lower counterpoint being in semiquavers almost throughout.

108. We must not, however, rush to the conclusion that *every* dissonance may now be freely used, if it can only be explained as part of a fundamental discord. It is needful also carefully to consider the resolution which is to follow. If, for example, we take the interval of the diminished seventh, and give it its ordinary resolution,

it is evident that if this be inverted in the octave, the perfect fifth will become a bare fourth, which we know (§ 102) is unallowable. If we employ a diminished seventh at all, we shall have to give it some other resolution; *e.g.*—

The student will see for himself the inversions of these passages. At the fourth crotchet of (*a*) we have taken a fourth as an accented passing note; and the inversion of (*b*) will give a fourth as an unaccented passing note; both these examples are quite correct. It must further be observed that the usual resolution of the diminished seventh, though unavailable for inversion in the octave, is quite practicable for either the tenth or the twelfth—

Inversion in the 10th.　　Inversion in the 12th.

109. The interval of the augmented sixth shows a somewhat similar case. In double counterpoint of the octave it should not be used at all—at all events in two parts—because of the harsh effect of its inversion, the diminished third; but its inversion in the tenth gives a diminished fifth, and in the twelfth a diminished seventh, both of which may be freely used, provided they are properly resolved—

Inversion in 8ve.   Ditto in 10th.   Ditto in 12th.

110. The admission of fundamental discords further lightens our labour in another way, especially with double counterpoint in the tenth and twelfth, by allowing us to use certain combinations which in strict counterpoint were unavailable because their inversions produced dissonances. For example, we saw in § 56 that in double counterpoint in the tenth we could not take a sixth above the subdominant, because its inversion gave us a diminished fifth. But in free counterpoint we can use this interval, *provided that the next note of the subject will allow us to resolve its inversion correctly.* An example will make this clear.

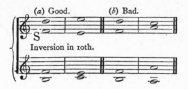

Inversion in 10th.

At (*a*) the diminished fifth in the inversion receives its proper resolution, at (*b*) it does not; the former progression is therefore good, the latter bad. In the same way, we may take a diminished fifth above the leading note in double counterpoint in the tenth (representing the first inversion of the dominant seventh), always provided that we can follow it properly.

111. Under similar limitations, we can employ some of the hitherto prohibited intervals in double counterpoint of the twelfth. A sixth can be used as a harmony note above either the subdominant, the tonic, or the submediant, because its inversion will give us in the first two cases the root position of either the dominant or supertonic seventh, and in the last the first inversion of the dominant ninth. For the same reason a sixth may be employed below the dominant, supertonic, or leading note; we can also take the octave above the subdominant, in either a major or minor key, and the octave above the submediant, or below the supertonic, in the minor key. But we cannot too strongly impress

on the student the fact that these intervals can in no case be used
when their dissonant inversions cannot be properly resolved.
With double counterpoint in the octave there will be no danger ;
because the inversion of a dissonance in the octave changes only
the position, not the nature of the chord.   With the tenth and
twelfth, as we know, it is quite different.

112. The restrictions as to melodic progressions in double
counterpoint of the tenth and twelfth (§§ 57, 58, 86) are still to
be enforced, with the one exception, that it is occasionally
possible in the free style to take an augmented second or an
augmented fourth in the melody, when both notes are part of the
same harmony.   This, however, will very seldom be necessary,
and the progression should be most sparingly used, if at all.

113. Free double counterpoint can be written either against
a subject in notes mostly of equal length, such as a choral or
hymn-tune ; or two florid parts can be written in double counterpoint with one another.   In actual composition the latter is by
far the more common ; but it will be best for the student to begin
by practising double counterpoint on a choral.   In doing this,
he should always endeavour to make his counterpoint as flowing
and melodious as he can, and remember that he is writing *music*,
and not solving mathematical problems on intervals.   We shall
now give, as patterns, double counterpoints in the octave, tenth,
and twelfth, on a well-known German choral.

114. We first write a double counterpoint in the octave—

E

As it is important to think of the implied harmony, it will be
well for the student to figure his basses throughout, as we have
done here. These counterpoints will repay close examination,
though they require but few explanations. At (*a*) will be seen in
the upper counterpoint an augmented fourth, and in the inversion
a diminished fifth, both representing the dominant seventh of
B minor. The transient modulation to the key of the relative
minor is here of excellent effect. At (*b*) a sharp is put in brackets
over the second quaver, G; this note can be either G♯ or G♮,
according to the harmony intended. *As the basses are here figured,*
we have an inverted cadence (*Counterpoint,* § 505) in B minor;
in this case the G must be natural. But it would be also possible, though less good here, to regard the chord as the submediant
of A major, not making a modulation to B minor at all; and in
this case G, being an auxiliary note above the harmony note, would
be sharp. At (*c*) and (*d*) we have indicated two chords as implied
above the bass note, so as to avoid the bad harmonic progression
II*a* to I*a*.

115. Double counterpoint in the tenth, though easier in the free style than in the strict, will be found considerably more difficult than that in the octave. We are, however, as has been shown above, much less restricted in our harmony, owing to our ability to use fundamental discords; and the permission given in § 59, to disregard implied root-progressions, must, therefore, now be withdrawn; for it will be quite impossible to write really good *musical* double counterpoint in the tenth unless we consider the harmony that is implied. We shall, therefore, for our next examples figure our basses, as we did with the last.

116. It must further be observed that we are now no longer absolutely debarred, as in the strict style, from the employment of similar motion; for we can now approach a third or a sixth by similar motion whenever its inversion will produce one of the allowed hidden fifths or octaves (*Harmony*, §§ 103, 105).

117. We now give a double counterpoint in the tenth on the choral we are treating. It will be seen to furnish much more material for comment than that in the octave—

At (*a*) the progression from a third to a fifth, which is mostly
bad in two parts moving by step, cannot well be avoided.
It must be noticed that this double counterpoint is seldom used
in two parts only ; as soon as a third part is added the bad effect
disappears.   At (*b*) we use the hitherto prohibited sixth above
the subdominant, the inversion of which is a diminished fifth,
because the next note of the subject allows us to resolve it correctly (§ 110).   At (*c*) we meet with a case of frequent occurrence.
Here we take the inversion in the key of B minor, while the
upper counterpoint remains for four bars longer in the original
key of D.   It would have been possible, by the omission of the
sharps to G and A, to keep the lower counterpoint in the key of
D ; but this would have been far less satisfactory, because the
harmony would have consisted almost entirely of the *weaker*
chords of that key, II., III., and VI., whereas by going into
B minor, we use all the *strong* chords, I., IV., and V.   It may
be laid down as a general principle that the larger the proportion
of the three strong chords of the key (the tonic, subdominant,
and dominant), the firmer and better the harmonic progression
will be.

118. At (*d*) we save the approach of a sixth (becoming in the
lower part a fifth), by similar motion, by going beyond the interval
and then returning.   It must be observed that it would have been
quite possible here to approach this sixth by similar motion, had
we desired it, because the hidden fifths in the lower parts are among
those that are permitted.   At (*e*) we take the sixth above the
leading note, instead of the here possible diminished fifth (§ 110),

because its inversion gives us a stronger harmonic progression in the lower part.

119. The figuring of the bass at (*f*) should be particularly noticed. We have indicated the second inversion of the dominant eleventh, because this chord is much better than a plain chord of the sixth on the supertonic to precede the chord of the dominant seventh. Observe also at (*g*) how the third inversion of the dominant seventh in the upper part gives the root position of the same chord when inverted in the tenth below. At (*h*) we have taken the dissonant G♯ in the bass instead of G♮, not only to avoid the augmented second, but to introduce the second inversion of the fundamental ninth on the supertonic, resolving it on the first inversion of the dominant seventh.

120. At (*i*) in the upper part we do not necessarily imply a doubled leading note. We may quite well consider the key of this bar to be A major, when the C sharp will be the doubled third of the tonic chord approached by step. At (*k*) we see the reverse procedure to that which we noticed at (*c*). Here the upper part modulates, while the lower remains in the original key. From (*l*) the first two lines of the choral are repeated. We have endeavoured here, as in the preceding counterpoint, to obtain as much variety of harmony and melody as possible. At (*m*) we make the cadence free in the bass, so as to get a better close.

121. Lastly, we write a double counterpoint in the twelfth against the same choral, and, in order to get more variety, we will take it in triple time—

At (*a*) the sixth above the subdominant is taken as a harmony
note (§ 111), its inversion in the bass giving a dominant seventh.
As we happen to have approached it by step, it would be possible
here to regard the E in the bass as an accented passing note;
but it is far better to consider it as a genuine seventh; the
harmonic progression is stronger. At (*b*) we indicate two chords
in the bar to save the bad progression II*a* to I*a*; the same thing
is seen two bars later.

122. The progression of the bass at (*c*) requires careful attention. Evidently the last quaver must be a harmony note; for
if we think of the submediant chord as being continued through
the bar, D will be a second passing note returning in the
following bar to the first one. If we here take D♮ instead of
D♯, we shall have the false relation of the tritone; but by using
the first inversion of the fundamental seventh on the supertonic,
we get out of all our difficulties. We have marked the $\frac{6}{5}$ under
the D♯ for the sake of clearness; but the harmony should of
course change at the beginning of the third crotchet, the E
being an accented passing note. In four parts we should fill up
the harmony, thus—

That no modulation is implied to the key of E is, of course,
shown by the contradiction of the D♯ in the following bar.

123. At (*d*) is a somewhat, though not precisely, similar point.
Here we are just going into the dominant key; if we take D♮
here, we have the false relation of the tritone, and the effect is
extremely harsh. As the preceding crotchet E is here a harmony
note, it would be possible to consider D as an auxiliary note;
but if we do this, it must still be D *sharp*, because it is below the
fifth of the chord (*Harmony*, § 248). At (*e*) we see a diminished
fifth in the bass, resulting from the inversion of the octave
above the subdominant. The apparently free treatment of the
dominant seventh here will be seen to be fully justified if we give

the harmonic outline, omitting the passing notes in the bass, and filling up the chords—

The chord of the seventh first changes its position ; and the seventh rises because the bass moves to the note of its resolution (*Harmony* §§ 216, 303). We are intentionally introducing the progressions which were forbidden in the strict style, to show how to manage them properly.

124. The $^{\sharp 6}_{5}$ marked in the bass at (*f*) is a parallel case to that which we have been examining at (*c*). The last quaver must imply a change of harmony, which (as before) should, of course, be taken at the third crotchet, D$\sharp$ being an accented passing note. The figuring here given represents the second inversion of the supertonic major ninth ; we have taken this in preference to the submediant triad, as the latter might easily imply consecutive fifths in a middle voice with the following chord. Note also that in this passage, as in some places of our double counterpoint in the tenth, the two counterpoints are in different keys, the upper one being in F$\sharp$ minor, and the lower in E major. In all double counterpoints in the tenth and twelfth, we may freely introduce accidentals, if we thereby obtain better melodic or harmonic progressions.

125. After what has been already said, the student will readily see why at (*g*) we have marked $\sharp 6$ under B. In the bass the modulation back from B minor to A is made one bar sooner, at (*h*). Here we have, exceptionally, three chords implied in the bar. On the repetition of the first part of the subject, we have, as in our previous examples, varied the counterpoint.

126. At (*i*) will be found another sixth treated as a harmony note—not one of the sixths, be it noticed, which we have allowed in § 111. We have introduced this one to illustrate our general rule that any dissonance may be used in free counterpoint, provided it clearly represents a fundamental discord (§ 104). Here the seventh below the dominant represents the fourth inversion of the dominant major thirteenth. The full harmony of this and the preceding bar will be

A fine example, from Beethoven, of the employment of this chord in the same position is given in *Harmony*, § 423. At (*k*) two chords are indicated below B, as before, because the next chord is I*a* ; and, lastly, from (*l*) the cadence is free (§ 88).

127. The student will now be prepared to write double counterpoint for himself on hymn-tunes and chorals. He can take any familiar tune for treatment, or, if he prefer chorals, he will find a selection of fifty, which will be admirably adapted for his purpose in the author's *Additional Exercises to Counterpoint.* But he will do well to remember that it is not every subject that is adapted for double counterpoint in the tenth. The choral we have been treating proved very suitable, though it was not selected for that reason. What we may describe as an *undulating* melody—one that alternately rises and falls—will be the easiest to manage in the tenth. But any melody can be fitted with a double counterpoint in the octave or twelfth by dint of patience and perseverance. It will be excellent practice to write one of each kind of double counterpoint on the same subject, as we have done in this chapter ; the student will thus obtain some insight into the almost inexhaustible resources of harmony.

CHAPTER VI.

FREE DOUBLE COUNTERPOINT ON A FLORID SUBJECT.

128. By the term "florid subject" is here meant any subject in which the notes are of no regular length, as distinguished from the chorals which have been treated of in the last chapter. We are not now restricting the work "florid" to the narrow sense in which it is frequently employed, as meaning rapid, or highly ornamented; but we are using it just as we do when we speak of the fifth species as "florid counterpoint." We have already said that this is by far the most common kind of counterpoint in actual composition; and we shall therefore in this chapter have the advantage of being able to draw our illustrations from the works of the great masters, instead of being obliged, as hitherto, to write all our own examples.

129. The general principles to be followed in writing this kind of double counterpoint are exactly the same as those which guide us in adding a double counterpoint to a choral; but there is one additional rule to be enforced, with which the student has already made acquaintance in working combined counterpoint. Let him remember the rule given in *Counterpoint*, § 407: "When two parts are in the fifth species, variety should be sought by taking longer notes in one of the parts against shorter notes in the other." To apply this rule in the present case, *the subject and counterpoint should be contrasted as much as possible, both in melody and rhythm.*

130. Double counterpoint in the octave is by far the most frequently employed and the most useful; next in order comes that in the twelfth, which is tolerably common. But double counterpoint in the tenth (probably owing to its difficulty) is extremely rare, and, excepting in pieces written expressly to illustrate it, is only to be met with incidentally, and generally for only a few notes.

131. The most frequent employment of double counterpoint of all kinds is in fugues, of which (as will be shown in the next volume of the present series) it forms one of the chief ingredients. But its utility is by no means restricted to this branch of composition. It frequently plays an important part in large instrumental works, such as symphonies and sonatas, and is even to be met with in vocal music which is not fugal. Illustrations of each kind will be given presently.

132. It will be most convenient to give first examples of double counterpoint in the octave, reserving those in the tenth and twelfth for a later part of the chapter; and we shall commence with some examples from the works of the greatest contrapuntist that the world has ever seen—Johann Sebastian Bach.

(1)   J. S. BACH.   " Wohltemperirtes Clavier," Fugue 30.

(2)

This passage requires hardly any explanation. At (2) we see the inversion, in a different key, of the passage at (1). By the simple rule given in § 8 it will at once be seen that the inversion is in the octave. Notice the contrast in rhythm and melody between the two subjects (§ 129).

133. Our next illustration

(1)   J. S. BACH.   Organ Fugue in C minor.

(2)

shows a case frequently met with. Here the inversion is not only in a different key, but in the major mode, instead of the minor. This evidently alters the character of the music, but the

intervals of inversion are still exactly maintained. It should be
mentioned that at (2) the double counterpoint is in the two
middle parts of a four-part harmony. We have not quoted the
outer parts, as double counterpoint with added parts will be
treated of in the next chapter.

134. The following extract from the two-part fugue in
E minor of the "Wohltemperirtes Clavier"

J. S. BACH. "Wohltemperirtes Clavier," Fugue 10.

illustrates some fresh points. Observe, first, that there is much
less contrast in the character of the two subjects than in the
examples hitherto given. This is because the fugue is a kind of
moto continuo, a special feature of which is the persistence of the
semiquavers from the first bar to the last. This passage also
illustrates what was said in the last chapter (§ 104), as to the
sounding of dissonant notes together. The semiquaver E in the
first bar of the bass is clearly an auxiliary note ; but at (*a*) are
evidently notes of the chord of the dominant eleventh (second
inversion), and at (*b*) we have the dominant seventh in the key
of D. The third and fourth bars of this passage are the inversion,
in the key of the dominant, of the first and second ; and the
augmented fourth at (*c*) represents the fourth inversion of the
dominant eleventh in D.

135. A similar point is illustrated in our next example—

J. S. BACH. Organ fugue in E minor.

Here the inversion is really in the twenty-second, or triple octave, the upper part being transposed two octaves lower, and at the same time the lower part an octave higher. But just as in harmony we speak of one note as being the octave of another, though it may be three or four octaves away, so we speak of double counterpoint in the octave, whatever the actual distance, if the relation of the two parts to one another harmonically is the same as if the transposition were really only one octave. (Compare §§ 13, 107.) At (*a*) in this example the augmented second represents the last inversion of a supertonic minor ninth, and the diminished fifth at (*b*) represents the second inversion of the augmented (French) sixth. In the inversion at (2) these two intervals give us at (*c*) and (*d*) the first inversion of the supertonic ninth, and the uninverted French sixth, thus exemplifying what we said in § 111—that the inversion of a dissonance in the octave changes only the position, and not the nature of a chord. At (*e*) two crotchets are substituted for four quavers for technical reasons ; here the bass is played on the pedals, and Bach has simplified the passage, as he often does in such a case.

136. We shall give more examples from Bach when we come to deal with double counterpoint in the tenth and twelfth, and also with added parts ; we will now take a few extracts from the works of Bach's greatest contemporary—Handel. Our first illustration

shows a very simple double counterpoint in the octave in the strict diatonic style. It is so straightforward as to require no explanation.

137. In our next example, taken from the grand chorus,
" From the censer,"

HANDEL. "Solomon."

the two subjects are first announced by the alto and tenor voices,
and immediately inverted by the soprano and bass, the former
entering before the end of the subject.   This passage illustrates at (*a*) the occasional possibility, in free writing, of the
crossing of the parts for a moment.   This, however, is a license
which the student is not recommended to imitate.

138. The following passage

HANDEL. " Susanna.

is given for the sake of comparison with the extract from Bach, quoted in § 132. In both cases, the most important feature is the descending chromatic scale. Notice what a different counterpoint is written against it by the two composers. At (*a*) will be seen a chromatic F♯ in the alto, which in the inversion at (*b*) becomes F ♮. Such chromatic alterations, though by no means infrequent in double counterpoint of the tenth and twelfth, are rather rare when the inversion is in the octave.

139. The last example that we shall give from Handel

shows how to obtain variety by contrast of melody and rhythm when both subjects are in notes of comparatively slow time. The D♯ at (*a*) of the inversion is another instance of the chromatic alteration of a note spoken of above. This will be oftener met with in Handel than in Bach.

140. With the older composers such double counterpoint as that which we have been quoting is mostly found in fugal writing. All the extracts we have given as yet have been from fugues, either instrumental or vocal. But in modern music the devices of double counterpoint are frequently used to impart additional interest to the development of the thematic material of a composition. Old "Father" Haydn, the founder of the modern school of instrumental writing, was one of the first to employ double counterpoint for this purpose; we give a few extracts from his works to illustrate the method of procedure.

141. One of his quartetts opens with the following subject—

In the second part of the movement the first notes of this theme are varied, and a double counterpoint in the octave added, thus—

It will be seen that the fourth and fifth bars of this passage are the inversion of the first and second. We omit the middle parts of the harmony, as the progression of the outer voices is not affected by them.

142. In the example just given, a counterpoint in quavers' is added to a subject in longer notes. Our next illustration will show the reverse process, a counterpoint of long notes being added to a subject in quavers. It is taken from the finale of Haydn's quartett in A, Op. 55, No. 1, the first theme of which is

In the course of the movement occurs the following passage, of which, for the sake of clearness, we give the score in full, numbering the bars for convenience of reference—

In bars 1 to 4 we see in the first violin a variation of the first
theme, to which in the violoncello is added a counterpoint in
semibreves and minims, the viola entering with a free part at the
second bar. From bars 5 to 8 we find the inversion in the
octave of bars 1 to 4. Note here that, in consequence of
the close position of the two voices, the first part of the counterpoint does not undergo inversion. We see it strictly inverted by
the viola and violoncello at bars 12 and 13. At bars 8 and 9 is a
curious and interesting variation of the counterpoint. In the
ninth bar the quaver figure which in bar 1 was used against the
first bar of the counterpoint is employed against the second, and
one bar of the continuation is consequently omitted. The whole
passage is a beautiful example of the application of double
counterpoint in practical composition.

143. The following passage from one of Haydn's earlier
symphonies shows the employment of double counterpoint in a
sequence—

F

As in previous examples, we have omitted the middle parts of the harmony.

144. Our last extract from Haydn is of an altogether different kind. It is the commencement of the slow movement of a symphony—

The first eight bars of this passage are in two-part harmony only, each part being doubled in the octave. At (*a*) the whole phrase is inverted, middle parts (not quoted) being added to fill up the harmonies.

145. Our first quotation from Mozart

(2)

strikingly illustrates the difference between strict and free counterpoint. In the strict style, the consecutive octaves between the first notes of the first and second bars, and the arpeggio of the chord of the dominant seventh in the fourth bar would be objectionable. Here they are quite allowable.

146. Our next example

MOZART. Symphony in G minor.

shows a case of not infrequent occurrence. We have here a counterpoint written on the first subject of the movement; the subject (as many readers will be aware) is that given in the bass of the first four bars. If we compare (*b*) of the inversion with (*a*) of the original counterpoint we shall see that a slight change in the figure is here made. This is to keep the parts in a comfortable compass. Had the counterpoint at (*b*) been an exact imitation of (*a*) the bass would have been inconveniently high; on the other hand, the figure of (*b*) could not have been employed at (*a*) without crossing the parts. Such small modifications may always be allowed in free double counterpoint.

147. The following charming little piece of double counterpoint

MOZART.
Variations on " Unser dummer Pöbel meint."

gives in the first four bars an example of free imitation, a subject
to be dealt with later in this volume (Chapter X.). As in a
previous example, we have numbered the bars. The inversion
begins at bar 9. Compare the upper part of bars 6 and 7 with
the bass of bars 14 and 15. At bar 14 we see bar 5 varied by
the addition of accidentals (compare §§ 138, 139); and in bar 15
we find in the upper voice the bass of bar 7 with accented
auxiliary notes (*appoggiature*).* The eight and sixteenth bars of
this passage are free.

* As we have not had occasion to use this word before, it may be well to
remind the student that an *appoggiatura* (Italian—a "leaning note") is an
accented auxiliary note placed at the distance of a second from a harmony note,
and of not less than half its value.

148. The following example

shows a different treatment of a sequence from that seen in
§ 143.   Here the pattern is set in the first two bars, and inverted
in the third and fourth; the whole passage is then repeated a
tone lower.

149. Our next extract requires few words—

The upper part of (1) shows the first subject of the slow movement, to which, on its resumption in the latter part of the piece
the counterpoint here quoted is added.

150. It is comparatively seldom that a long passage of double
counterpoint is to be found in a scherzo; the following is an
excellent example—

BEETHOVEN. Sonata, Op. 26.

Notice at (*b*) the alteration of one note of the subject at (*a*).

151. A charming combination of two melodies strongly contrasted in character is to be seen in the following extract from the first movement of Cherubini's second string quartett—

CHERUBINI. Quartett in C.

As before, we omit the middle parts of the harmony.

152. Among the composers of the first half of the present century Mendelssohn and Schumann were probably the greatest contrapuntists. It is seldom, nevertheless, that we find double counterpoint developed at any great length in their works, especially in those of Schumann. We give two examples from Mendelssohn, totally differing from one another in character—

The overture to "St. Paul," from which the above passage is taken, is in the contrapuntal style throughout; but there are not many bars which are *strictly* inverted. Even in this extract it will be noticed that the last group of semiquavers is free, and the inversion only lasts for a little more than two bars.

153. Every one who has heard the "Scotch" symphony will remember the beautiful effect produced in the first movement by the combination of two of the chief themes.

154. Our last example of double counterpoint in the octave will be from a work by a living composer, Johannes Brahms—

BRAHMS. "Deutsches Requiem."

This fine passage illustrates the tendency of the modern school toward freedom in contrapuntal writing. It will be seen that in the second bar of this extract, the fifth crotchet, at (*a*) is altered in the inversion at (*b*). (Compare § 150.) The last bar of the passage, also, though maintaining a general resemblance, is not a strict inversion at (2) of the model. It is difficult to give a satisfactory reason why any change should have been made here ; but it may be said, once for all, that in modern compositions good specimens of strictly inverted double counterpoint are far more rarely to be met with than in the works of the old masters.

155. We have several times noticed the rarity of the employment of double counterpoint in the tenth, as compared with those in the octave and twelfth. In the whole of Bach's "Forty-Eight Preludes and Fugues" it is very seldom met with, *e.g.*, in fugues Nos. 29, 40, and 45 ; though double counterpoint in the twelfth is tolerably frequent, and that in the octave is to be found in every fugue. In our first chapter we quoted passages from two of the fugues we have named (§§ 9, 11) ; we will therefore give for our present illustrations some extracts from Bach's "Art of Fugue," the tenth number of which is specially written to exemplify double counterpoint in the tenth, of which it is probably the finest specimen ever composed. The two subjects to be combined are in the first instance worked separately, and are not found together until the 44th bar, when they appear thus—

We first see them inverted in the following manner in bar 52—

The alteration of the first note in this passage is necessitated by the laws of fugal construction.   If the student will compare these two examples, he will see, with the guidance given him in §§ 8, 9, that the inversion here is in the tenth.   The next inversion (bar 66) will make this even clearer—

By comparing (c) with (a) it will be seen that the lower part of (c) is the upper part of (a), an octave lower; while the upper part of (c) is the lower part of (a), a tenth higher.

156. When treating of double counterpoint in the tenth, we mentioned (§ 80) that it differed from all other kinds, in the fact that it could be used simultaneously in two parts, which would move in thirds, sixths, or tenths, according to their positions. Our next extracts will illustrate this (bar 75)—

Compare this with (c), and we shall observe that the two outside parts are inverted in the octave, and therefore in the tenth of the original model at (a).   The middle part makes with the bass exactly the same intervals which the two parts made at (a); and were it inverted with the bass, we should have double

counterpoint in the *octave*.   In our next example, the thirds are
added to the other subject (bar 86)—

157. Let the student compare this passage with (*a*).   He will
see that the middle voice gives the inversion in the tenth, and
the thirds above it now give the inversion in the *twelfth*.   In
example (*d*) the added part would have inverted in the octave.
Thirds or sixths added to a double counterpoint in the tenth will
produce double counterpoint in the octave or twelfth, according
to the position.

158. The last passage we shall quote (bar 104)—

shows the inversion of (*e*).   By comparing it with (*a*), it will be
seen that here, as at (*d*), we have simultaneous counterpoint
in the tenth and octave.   These various counterpoints show how
both the subjects can be transposed.   It will be remembered
that in § 79 the student was told not to transpose his *canto fermo*;
but when, as here, the two parts are of equal importance, it is
possible, as we see, to transpose either of them.

159. It will be noticed that in none of the passages we have
given are the thirds or sixths added to both subjects at once.
This, however, would have been possible, and is not infrequently
done.   An excellent example of this will be seen in the great
fugue, in G minor, of the "Wohltemperirtes Clavier."   The
subject and counterpoint, with their original inversion in the
octave, were given at (*a*) and (*b*) of § 10.   At the 59th bar of
the fugue, we find the following—

J. S. BACH.   " Wohltemperirtes Clavier," Fugue 40.

Here thirds are added both to the subject and counter-subject.
By comparing the voices with those of the model in § 10,

we shall see that we have simultaneously double counterpoint
in the octave between the alto and tenor, in the tenth between
soprano and tenor and alto and bass, and in the twelfth between
soprano and bass. Such thirds can be added to any double
counterpoint in the octave, provided that similar motion and
an unprepared sixth are avoided, the former being, as we know,
unavailable in double counterpoint in the tenth, and the latter in
the twelfth.

160. In the third volume of Albrechtsberger's theoretical
works will be found two fugues written in double counterpoint
in the tenth; but as extracts from these would show little or
nothing which has not been already illustrated in the examples
we have just given from Bach, we content ourselves with referring students to Albrechtsberger's treatise. We will now
give a few passages in which double counterpoint in the tenth
is incidentally used. These will mostly be very short, as it is but
seldom that an opportunity occurs for the employment of this
device.

161. Handel scarcely ever writes double counterpoint at
this interval. A fragment, of only half a bar's length, will be
seen in the following passage—

At (*b*) is shown the inversion in the tenth of (*a*).

162. Our next example shows how double counterpoint in the
tenth can be obtained by adding thirds or tenths to that in the
octave—

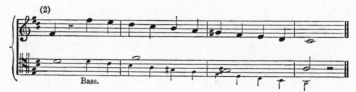

Here the regular double counterpoint of the fugue is, as usual, in the octave. This inversion is shown in the small notes of (2); but the bass is here accompanied by the treble in tenths, the latter thus giving double counterpoint in the tenth against the subject.

163. In the following passage,

the two subjects are mostly worked in the octave; but an incidental double counterpoint in the tenth is introduced, as shown at (2). If the student will examine these two subjects, he will see that they would also be capable of inversion in the twelfth.

164. In instrumental music, double counterpoint in the tenth is even rarer than in vocal. We give a very short specimen by Mozart—

It will be noticed that only the first eight notes of this counterpoint are really inverted in the tenth.   By a slight modification of
the figure, Mozart changes the interval of inversion to the octave.

   165. The scarcity of illustrations must be the author's
apology for introducing an example from his own pen—

E. Prout.   Symphony in D, No. 4.

   166. We conclude our illustrations of this counterpoint with
a portion of the masterly canon in the tenth in Bach's " Art of
Fugue "—

J. S. Bach.   " Art of Fugue."

This wonderful movement is too long to quote in full; but a
somewhat extended extract is required to make it intelligible.
We number the bars for the sake of reference. The subject of
canon will be spoken of later in this volume; it will suffice now
to say that a canon is a composition in which one part continuously
imitates another at any given interval. In the present case it will
be seen that the upper voice imitates the lower at a distance of
four bars, and at the interval of a tenth above. We give only the
first half of the canon, which is continued strictly to the 39th bar.
From the 44th bar to the end of the piece, with the exception of
the last four bars, which are free, the whole canon is inverted in
double counterpoint of the tenth.

167. Let the student first examine the model, bars 5 to 21.
The counterpoint begins at bar 5, and it will be seen that in the
harmony considerable prominence is given to the intervals of the
fifth and sixth, which in the inversion become respectively the
sixth and fifth. Observe that in the exposition, so to speak, of
the canon, Bach, at bars 9 to 12, inverts bars 5 to 8 in the tenth.
In bar 18, at the second crotchet, is a diminished fifth struck by
the two parts. This is because it clearly represents the first
inversion of a dominant seventh (§ 104). In bars 13 and 14
will be seen sixths approached by similar motion, from accent to
accent; the inversion produces hidden fifths (bars 52, 53).
Though these would be objectionable in strict counterpoint,
they may be allowed in free, especially in double counterpoint
in the tenth, in accordance with the often mentioned general
principle, that in proportion as the difficulty of the task increases,
the strictness of the rules in less important points is relaxed.
Similar hidden fifths will be seen in the example to § 165.

168. Now let us look at the inversion, bars 44 to 60. If we
compare the commencement of the canon (bars 1 to 4) with the
upper of the two subjects of the fugue given in § 155, we shall
see that the former is a variation of the latter. Both are, in fact,
varied forms of the *canto fermo*, on which, either direct or by
inverse movement, the whole of the "Art of Fugue" is
composed.

Subject.   Inversion.

In the canon, as in the fugue, it is the inverted form of the
subject which is taken for treatment; but it will be noticed that

in all the examples quoted from the fugue (§§ 155 to 158), it is the lower part which is transposed a tenth higher, while in the canon it is the upper part which is transposed a tenth lower.   Moritz Hauptmann, in his Analysis of the " Art of Fugue," has called attention to this, and given, undoubtedly, the true reason, that the original subject (the upper part at § 155 (*a*), and the lower part in the canon) is really the *canto fermo*, which therefore must not be transposed (§ 79).   At bars 48 to 51, we see again the inversion in the tenth of the four preceding bars, with the curious result that bars 48 to 51 are identical with bars 5 to 8 of the model.   The whole of this extract deserves close examination, comparing the inversion bar by bar with the model.

169. Double counterpoint in the twelfth, though somewhat less rare than that in the tenth, is yet far from common, especially with modern writers.   The examples now to be given will sufficiently illustrate its practical use—

In the inversion, we have added the upper voice, which is in thirds with the bass, because it does not obscure the clearness of the counterpoint.   Notice at (*a*) and (*b*) sixths in the pattern, the inversions of which at (*c*) and (*d*) become fundamental sevenths, and compare §§ 104, 111.

170. Our next illustration is very similar in character—

Here, again, the sixth can be taken at (*a*), because the inversion at (*b*) gives us the dominant seventh on C♯.

171. The following passage

(1) Bars 27—30.　　　　　　BACH. " Wohltemperirtes Clavier," Fugue 47.

(2) Bars 42—45.

shows how the inversion in the third bar produces a modulation to the key of the relative minor. Similar cases were seen in the counterpoints on a choral in the tenth and twelfth which we gave in the last chapter.

172. Our next example is taken from the fugue, written by Bach, in his "Art of Fugue," expressly to illustrate double counterpoint in the twelfth—

(1)　　　　　　　　　　　BACH. " Art of Fugue," No. 9.

G

At (1) we see in the upper voice the *direct* form of the subject quoted in § 168, the inversion of which was used for double counterpoint in the tenth. At (2) is the inversion of the counterpoint in the twelfth. Compare (*a*) with (*c*), and (*b*) with (*d*), and notice particularly the alterations in the position of the semitones. Had the scale passage at (*a*) been exactly imitated at (*b*), there would have been a modulation to the key of A minor, which Bach did not wish. Such chromatic alterations of notes will be more often met with in a minor than in a major counterpoint. In the last three bars of this example, where the music modulates to the key of the relative major, the only note altered in the inversion is the leading note (§ 84).

173. The following passage, taken from one of Handel's "Chandos Anthems,"

exemplifies a somewhat different point. Here the inversion begins in the twelfth. The sixth above the subject at (*a*) becomes in the inversion, not a fundamental seventh, as in the examples to §§ 169, 170, but an accented passing note (§ 85). Observe that at (*b*), in the third bar, further inversion in the twelfth becomes impracticable ; the rest of the passage, from (*d*), is therefore inverted in the octave.

174. Sometimes more than one part may be inverted at once—

In this example, we have at (2) omitted the tenor part, which is free, to show the inversions more clearly. The subject, which at (1) is in the treble, is at (2) in the bass. The alto, which at (1)

began on the fifth below the subject, begins at (2) on the octave above, and it is therefore inverted in the twelfth. At the same time the tenor, which in the model began on the tenth below the subject, begins (now in the treble) in the inversion on the tenth (= the third) above, and is therefore likewise in double counterpoint in the twelfth.

175. The double fugue in Mozart's "Requiem" has probably been quoted in every book on double counterpoint published since it was composed. It is, nevertheless, too fine an example to be omitted here—

The two themes announced at (1) are first inverted in the octave, as at (2), and subsequently in the twelfth, as at (3). Notice how, as in previous examples, the inversion of a sixth becomes a dominant seventh. We omit, as in many other examples, the accompanying parts.

176. Double counterpoint in the twelfth is not very frequently employed by Beethoven. The following example will require no explanation—

177. For our last example we give an entire movement, by one of Bach's most distinguished pupils, J. P. Kirnberger,

which is written throughout (excepting the free close, four bars in
length) in double counterpoint in the twelfth.   This very fine
specimen is taken from Clementi's " Practical Harmony "—

J. P. KIRNBERGER.

Inversion in the 12th.

That the student may the more readily compare the inversion with the model, we have numbered the bars in both, from 1 to 36. The bars at the end, from 37 to 40, give the free close, which (§ 88) is always a necessity with this counterpoint.

178. This example illustrates nearly all the rules we have given for double counterpoint in the twelfth. Observe that it begins with the interval of the octave—not with the fifth, as we have done in our examples. This is because the *upper* part is considered as the subject, and the lower as the counterpoint. This is clearly shown by the inversion, in which the lower part is transposed a twelfth higher, and not the upper part a twelfth lower. Notice also the great prominence given to the interval of the third, not only on the accented notes of the bar, but in successions of thirds (bars 17, 18, and 29 to 31). At bars 9 to 14 will be seen a good example of the sixth as a harmony note, prepared in the lower voice (§ 100), which in the inversion becomes a regularly prepared seventh. It will be seen that accidentals are freely used in the inversion (§ 124), if the melodic or harmonic progressions are thereby improved, as, for instance, in bars 29 to 31. The smooth flow of the whole counterpoint, in spite of the restrictions under which it is written, shows the composer to have been a worthy pupil of his illustrious master.

179. There is a spurious kind of double counterpoint, frequently to be found even in the works of the great masters, which must not be confounded with that which we are now treating of. It is not uncommon to meet with a theme accompanied by a more or less elaborate counterpoint above it (or below it, as the case may be), and then to find the theme accompanied in the reverse position by another counterpoint, bearing a general resemblance to the first, but not identical with it. Such counterpoint may be described as "electroplated" double counterpoint—very useful, often even artistic and beautiful; but after all only an inferior substitute for the genuine metal. It is naturally far easier to write, and very often for all practical purposes quite as effective ; but it must be taken for what it really is—counterpoint—*good* counterpoint, in most cases, but not *double* counterpoint.

180. That we may not be suspected of intending to disparage the counterpoint of which we are now speaking, we give two excellent examples of it—

(1)   HAYDN. "Creation.

It will be seen that the counterpoint of the second bar of (2) is not an inversion of the corresponding bar of the model, though it sounds sufficiently like it to be mistaken for it by a casual hearer. It is quite as effective as the real inversion would be—perhaps even more so ; and Haydn, doubtless, had good reasons for making the alteration, since nobody could write better double counterpoint than he when he chose.

181. Our second example is from Mendelssohn, indisputably one of the finest contrapuntists of the present century—

Here the figures of quavers, playing round the subject, are equally effective and charming in the first and second violins ; but they are not identical. It will be seen that each time the melody is above the counterpoint; we have, nevertheless, quoted the passage, because, as the student will easily see, both phrases are really written in double counterpoint in the octave, though neither is strictly inverted in the course of the movement.

182. It will be seen that nearly the whole of this long chapter is taken up with the analysis of examples. The resources of double counterpoint are so exhaustless that it is quite impossible to lay down precise rules as to every point that may occur. All that can be done is to indicate the general principles which should guide the student in writing, and to inculcate their observance by showing the practice of the great composers. Experience will do the rest. We have here taken but a few gleanings from the ample field of musical literature ; he who will take the trouble to explore it more thoroughly will

reap a large reward for his pains.   In double counterpoint, Bach is the unrivalled master of all masters.   Let those who would thoroughly understand this branch of their art, follow the advice of Schumann, and "let the 'Forty-eight Preludes and Fugues' be their daily bread."   Careful analysis of these works will teach the earnest student far more than he can learn from this, or any similar book.

183. The student should now begin to write free counterpoint in the octave, tenth, and twelfth for himself.   If he can, it will be best for him to invent both melodies ; but if he at first feels himself unequal to this, he will find a selection of subjects which will serve his purpose in the third and fifth sections of Part I. of the author's "Additional Exercises to *Counterpoint.*"

CHAPTER VII.

DOUBLE COUNTERPOINT WITH FREE PARTS ADDED.

184. We have frequently referred to the addition of other parts to two parts which were written in double counterpoint ; and in many of the examples given in the last chapter we have said that such parts were in the original, though they are omitted in our illustrations for the sake of showing the double counterpoints themselves more clearly. As a matter of fact, by far the larger number of double counterpoints are accompanied by what are called "free" parts, that is, by parts written only in simple, not in double, counterpoint with the others. When actual two-part double counterpoint is found without such additions, it is mostly at the beginning of a fugue, or in old music intended for the harpsichord, as in the examples from Bach and Kirnberger given in §§ 166, 177. We now proceed to show how one or more free parts are to be added to an existing double counterpoint.

185. The task now before the student differs from those which have hitherto engaged his attention in one important respect. In all the counterpoint he has yet worked, whether simple or double, he has always had one given subject to which to add one or more parts. Now, however, the two voices of the double counterpoint may be regarded as two *canti fermi*, to which one or more florid counterpoints have to be added. His work will now be very similar to that which he has had in some of the varieties of combined florid counterpoint.

186. It will be seen at once that the fact of there being two given subjects instead of one considerably limits the choice of harmony. In his very first attempts at counterpoint the student was told (*Counterpoint*, § 62) to consider the harmonic possibilities of each note of his subject. Thus, in the key of C, the note C may be the root of the tonic, the third of the submediant, or the fifth of the subdominant triads. As we are now dealing with free counterpoint, the same note may also be the seventh of the fundamental discord on the supertonic, or the eleventh of the chord of the dominant eleventh. Similarly F may be the root of the subdominant chord, the third of the diatonic triad on the supertonic, or the seventh of the dominant. But if the two notes of the double counterpoint, which are sounded together are F and C, several of the chords just named are at once

excluded.   We can neither take the tonic nor submediant triads,
nor the fundamental seventh on the supertonic, because F is not
a note of any of these chords.   So also, C does not belong to
the triad on the supertonic, nor the chord of the dominant
seventh.   With these two notes given, we are therefore practically
restricted to the subdominant triad or some position of the chord
of the dominant eleventh as our only available harmonies.

187. It is from such limitations as these that the student's
chief difficulties will arise, especially when he is adding a new
bass below both the given parts.   But in this case he must be
careful   not   to   hamper   himself   needlessly.   Supposing,   for
example, that   the two notes of his double counterpoint in the
key of C, are E and C, making a sixth between them, and that
he is going to add a bass, or perhaps a tenor and bass below
them.   The notes given suggest, of course, the first inversion of
the tonic chord ; but it would be a great mistake for the student
to imagine that the tonic harmony is the only one possible.   The
following example will soon convince him of this.   We give the
sixth in the upper parts, and add a tenor and bass below—

188. At (*a*) we give the tonic chord, as that which would
naturally occur first to the student.   This might also be taken in
the first inversion, and even in the second, if the context allowed
of its proper treatment.   At (*b*) and (*c*) are the root position and
first inversion of the submediant triad.   All these positions can
be used freely, and there would be little or no difficulty about
their introduction.   But it would be also possible to treat the
given notes, under certain circumstances, as parts of fundamental
discords.   At (*d*) (*e*) and (*f*) are shown various positions of the
supertonic major ninth.   These, of course, would be only available if the seventh and ninth could be properly resolved, and the
third of the supertonic chord were able to move a semitone
(*Harmony*, § 321).   At (*g*) and (*h*) are shown two positions of
the dominant thirteenth, and at (*i*) the tonic minor thirteenth,
any one of which would be at least possible.   It will be seen
that here are nine combinations of which the notes C and E
could form a part, and this list is not exhaustive.   The student's
resources, therefore, are not so limited after all as would appear
at first sight.

189. A very important consideration will always be, which
notes of the subject are to be treated as harmony notes, and

which as auxiliary or passing notes? It is impossible to lay down any absolute rules on this point; experience will be the student's best guide; but he must remember that he is now not restricted to one chord in a bar, or even to one chord against each note of his subject. He may change his harmony as often as he finds it expedient; and it will frequently happen that the interposition of a second chord will save a weak or bad root-progression.

190. It must also be borne in mind that we can now treat any note, accented or unaccented, whether approached by step or by leap, as an auxiliary note, *provided it is quitted by step.* In many cases this permission will be found extremely useful. The rule prohibiting the sounding of dissonant notes together, except when taken by step, is also to a very considerable extent relaxed; though judgment will need to be exercised in this matter, so as to avoid harshness as much as possible.

191. We shall now give a series of examples, to illustrate the principles we have laid down; from the careful analysis of these the student will, it is hoped, learn all that it will be needful for him to know. Following our usual method, we will take one short subject, and treat it in many different ways. For this purpose we will choose the first eight bars of the double counter-point in the octave which we worked on a choral in § 114.

192. We will first add a free middle part to the counterpoint. In order to do this, it will be necessary to transpose the lower voice an octave, to make room—

In all our examples we shall indicate by a "D. C." the two parts which are in double counterpoint with one another. We

choose an added middle part for our first example, as being
on the whole the easiest to work.   The only remarks to make
upon this example are, that at (*a*) there are not consecutive
octaves between treble and alto, because the crotchet A is a note
of the harmony; and that at (*b*) two chords are used on the
bass note.

193. We now take the double counterpoint in the two lower
parts of the harmony, and add a free part above—

We have here transposed the upper part of the double counterpoint an octave to get a better position for the harmony.   This
example might have been written, like the last, in the key of D,
giving the lower parts to tenor and bass, and the new part, a fifth
lower than written, to the alto.   We have preferred, for the sake
of comparison, to give all our three-part examples for treble, alto,
and bass voices.   Observe that the E♯ at (*a*) makes no false
relation with the E♮ of the alto of the preceding bar, because
the latter is a passing note.

194. We next add an upper part to the inversion of this
counterpoint—

A florid bass, such as is seen here, usually necessitates more changes of the harmony. In the second bar of this example, there are distinctly four chords. At (*a*) is a point worthy of notice. It looks at first sight as if the bass leapt to a second inversion from the inversion of another chord. So it does, if we choose to consider the third and fourth quavers of the bass as each representing different harmony. But in the free style in which we are now writing, we are not bound to assume this. We may look at the four quavers of the first minim as representing the supertonic chord—B and E being harmony notes, and C and D passing notes, as also would be the C in the treble ; or, instead of this, the A in the bass may be regarded as an ornamental note interposed between the E and D. That we have not, in spite of appearances, a true second inversion here, is shown by the fact that it is neither followed by another chord on the same bass note, nor by a chord on the next degree of the scale (*Harmony*, § 165). The only other harmony possible above the A and F would have been the first inversion of the mediant chord, from which the progression to the tonic at the fourth crotchet would have been weak. This passage illustrates the liberty which is allowed in free counterpoint, such as this.

195. It will generally be found more difficult to add a new bass below a double counterpoint than to add upper or middle parts. The following examples will show how this is to be managed—

At (*a*) is seen a somewhat, though not precisely, analogous
example of the introduction of a second inversion to that which
we have just been considering.   Here we can either call the F in
the bass a passing note, in which case the root progression is IV*a*
to V*c*; or we can look on the G as a passing note, both in treble
and bass, and regard the F as the harmony note, the progression
then being I*b* to V*c*.

196. We now put a bass below the inversion of the
counterpoint—

This example requires no explanation; but the student should
notice that, though the two upper parts are (except in relative
position) identical with those of the last example, every bar of
the bass—except, of course, the final tonic—is different from the
preceding.   It would have been possible to make the same bass
do duty below the counterpoint in its new position.   We have
written a fresh bass, to show that variety can be obtained, even
with the restrictions under which we are now writing.

197. We will now add two free parts to our counterpoint.
This is naturally rather more difficult than adding only one.   We
will begin with the easiest position, in which the additional parts
are the middle voices—

At (*a*) there is no second inversion of the submediant chord; if there were, the bass could not leap to the next note. There is here the resolution of a double suspension on the tonic chord, and the B in the treble is only a passing note. At (*b*) the alto and tenor parts cross for one crotchet, to save the octaves with the bass on the unaccented beats which would result if the alto part were—

(Compare *Counterpoint*, § 175.)

198. We next add two upper parts—

At (*a*) the G♯ of the tenor, being an auxiliary note, makes no false relation with the G♮ of the alto. A somewhat similar

example from Bach will be seen in *Harmony*, § 262. Here, however, the effect is much less harsh than in the passage cited,
partly because it is here in a middle voice, but chiefly because it
returns to the harmony note before the chord changes, which in
the extract from Bach it does not. The cadence at (*b*) is not
very comfortable ; this cannot be helped, as it arises from the low
position of the two given parts.

199. In our next example the double counterpoint is in the
alto and bass, with one free part above, and one in the middle—

The only remark to make on this example is that at (*a*) we have
varied the cadence given in the example to § 193, and intentionally sounded two dissonant notes together in the treble and
alto, to show that they can be thus taken, because they form part
of the chord of the dominant thirteenth (§ 104).

200. Our next examples illustrate the most difficult combinations—

Here two parts are added below the counterpoints. Note the firm progression of the new bass, resulting from the almost exclusive employment of the strong chords, I., IV., and V., of the keys of A and F♯ minor (§ 117).

201. Lastly we take the double counterpoint in the two middle voices, adding a treble and a bass—

This example needs no explanation.

202. We have now added free parts in ten different ways to the same phrase of eight bars; and if the student will compare them, he will see that no two are alike. There is necessarily a general resemblance of character about all, because our choice of harmony is so restricted; but there is quite sufficient diversity

H

of detail to show how much variety is possible, even with simple harmonies. It will be seen that no chromatic chords are employed in any of the examples; this is because the melody of the choral is so diatonic that chromatic harmony would have been entirely out of keeping with it. But to those who have the resources of harmony at their fingers' ends—and it may be presumed that no others will essay such advanced work as that which forms the subject of this volume—there never need be the least danger of monotony. Even the seven diatonic notes of the key furnish an exhaustless supply of harmonies to those who know how to use them.

203. It is possible to write free parts which shall themselves be in double counterpoint with the two given parts, and, in at least one standard work of counterpoint, exercises of this kind are set. In reality, however, these are of little practical use; because if a composer wishes to add such a part, he will most probably (and had better) make triple counterpoint at once. How this is to be done will be shown in a subsequent chapter.

204. It would have been considerably easier to add plain chords to our double counterpoint instead of florid parts. We have chosen the latter as being not only musically more interesting, but far more instructive to the student The more complete command he can acquire of all the varieties of florid counterpoint, the better equipped he will be for the work of practical composition.

205. The addition of free parts will often improve a progression that would be harsh or stiff in two parts only. For example, in our double counterpoint in the tenth in § 117 is seen between the first and second bars of the lower counterpoint a third followed by a fifth, with both parts moving by step. The uncomfortable effect disappears as soon as a free part is added, either above, in the middle, or below—

206. In the same way that which in two parts looks like the false relation of the tritone can often be saved. Thus, in § 67, the third and fourth bars of the example can be mended, in *free* counterpoint—and we need no longer confine ourselves to strict—as follows—

207. We shall conclude this chapter with a few examples of the addition of free parts to double counterpoints by the great masters; and, as the most instructive course we can pursue, we will show how several of the double counterpoints quoted in the last chapter were filled up by their composers. We first take the two passages from Bach's Organ Fugue in C minor given in § 133. Bach fills them up thus—

At (1) the added voices are the soprano and tenor, and, as the bass remains, the general effect of the harmony is much the same as in the outline previously given. But at (2) outside parts are added, and the new bass gives a totally different character to the music. Notice, especially, how in the third bar at the first crotchet the weak effect of the two-part harmony is improved by the additional voices.

208. In the extract from Bach's Organ Fugue in E minor given in § 135, the passage (1) is in two parts originally. The inversion at (2) appears in the following form—

Here nothing but plain chords are added; the filling up is less contrapuntal than in our last example. Observe the fine and unexpected effect of the chord of the dominant thirteenth in the third bar.

209. The example from Handel's "Susanna" in § 138 is somewhat similar. Here (1) is also in two parts only; at (2) a middle part is added—

Note that the sequential character of the treble and tenor is maintained in the added alto part. The upper part, as here given, is obviously too high for a chorus. Handel modifies it somewhat in the voice part; it is the first violin part, in which the inversion is exactly retained, which is quoted here.

210. We next show the filling up of the example from Beethoven in § 149—

53666

This passage illustrates what was said in § 203. If the added middle part of (1) and upper part of (2) be compared, they will be seen to be identical, except that the last three notes in the second passage are lowered an octave. The added part is in double counterpoint with the upper part of (1). Notice that it is possible to use the fourth here in the second bar (becoming a perfect fifth in the inversion), because there is another voice below it. We have no triple counterpoint here, because the added part cannot be used as a bass; if it be, we shall have at the beginning of the third bar a $\frac{6}{4}$ taken by leap from the inversion of another chord.

211. Our next illustration is somewhat similar: it is the completion of the passage from Cherubini given in § 151—

In both these passages we have three-part harmony only; in (1) the first violin is silent, while in (2) the two violins play in octaves throughout. The added middle part is here written in double counterpoint to both the others; the slight modifications at (2) are evidently made for the sake of getting more complete harmony.

212. We now give two examples of the filling up of a double counterpoint in the tenth. We first take that shown at (a) of § 155—

J. S. BACH. "Art of Fugue," No. 10.

Here, as in (2) of § 207, two outer parts are added. The passage requires no explanation, but, like all the other examples we are giving, will repay close examination.

213. In the inversion shown at § 155 (*b*) the added parts are the treble and tenor—

J. S. BACH.   "Art of Fugue," No. 10.

214. Lastly we shall give two examples of added parts to double counterpoint in the twelfth. We first take that quoted in § 171 from Bach's "Wohltemperirtes Clavier." At (1) the counterpoint is as we have given it, in two parts only; but at (2) it is completed thus—

J. S. BACH.   "Wohltemperirtes Clavier," Fugue 47.

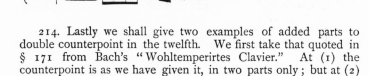

Here the added parts are the tenor and bass.

215. Our concluding example will be from Mozart's "Requiem"; the outline of which was seen in the three passages given in § 175. Of these that marked (1) is, as there shown, in two voices only; numbers (2) and (3) are filled up in the following manner—

In the first of these passages the double counterpoint is in the
bass and alto; in the second it is in the treble and bass, two
middle parts being added. Observe in the last bar but one
of (2) how the inversion in the twelfth of the interval of the sixth
in the pattern is used as a dominant seventh.

216. The student will now be prepared to practise the
writing of additional parts to double counterpoints for himself.
He will find it a very useful exercise to complete the counterpoint given in § 114 in all the ten ways in which we have worked
the first eight bars for him in §§ 192–201. He can then take the
double counterpoints we have given in §§ 117, 121, and treat
them in the same way. After this, if he desires more practice,
he may take any of the two-part examples from the works of the
great masters given in Chapter VI., and try to add free parts of
his own to them in all the various positions. Or, if he prefer it,
he can first write for himself two parts in double counterpoint in
the octave, tenth, or twelfth, and then add free parts. He will
find ample material in the examples we have given for as many
exercises as he is likely to want.

CHAPTER VIII.

DOUBLE COUNTERPOINT IN THE RARER INTERVALS.

217. Although, as has been more than once said, the only double counterpoints in common use are those in the octave, tenth, and twelfth, it is also possible to write counterpoints which will invert at the other intervals. There are, however, as will ·be seen directly, such difficulties connected with all these, as to render them practically useless, except incidentally. So far as we know, no compositions exist in which double counterpoints in the ninth, eleventh, thirteenth, or fourteenth are used systematically, as are those which have been already considered. It is, indeed, quite probable that where they are to be found, their occurrence is the result of accident, rather than of design. It would, therefore, be useless to give the student any rules for writing such counterpoints; but, for the sake of completeness, and as musical curiosities, we shall in this chapter give a few examples of each variety.

218. I. *Double counterpoint in the ninth.* One of the rarest and most unmanageable of all. The table of inversions in the ninth will evidently be the following—

INTERVALS: 1 2 3 4 5 6 7 8 9

INVERSIONS: 9 8 7 6 5 4 3 2 1

An examination of this table shows at once where the difficulty lies. Every consonance except the fifth becomes a dissonance when inverted; and although we have several times seen, in working our double counterpoints in the octave, tenth, and twelfth, how a harmony note may become a passing note in the inversion, and, *vice versâ*, it is very evident that if we have to treat every harmony note, except the fifth, in this way, our difficulties will be enormously increased. That it is, nevertheless, possible to write short passages in this counterpoint will appear from the specimens now to be given.

219. Our first example is by Marpurg—

In this very ingenious example, it will be seen that, excepting with the first and last notes, every consonance in one part is a prepared dissonance in the other. This counterpoint can also be inverted by transposing the subject a ninth higher, in which case it would be better to sharpen the C's, and thus take the music into the key of D.

220. Our next illustration is taken from Lobe's " Composition," Vol. III.—

The inversion in the bass is in the original an octave lower than here given, so as to leave room for the subsequent addition of free parts. It is here put at the real interval of a ninth below the model.

221. We shall give later in this chapter (§ 236) a very fine example from Bach, in which double counterpoints in the ninth and fourteenth are employed simultaneously. We now give a specimen by Beethoven—

BEETHOVEN.   Mass in D.

Here the counterpoint at (*b*) is clearly a repetition of that at (*a*), but at a different interval; for the first interval, which before was a seventh, is now a sixth, and so on with the others.   Whenever both counterpoints are above (as here), or both below, it is necessary to invert one of them in the octave, in order to find the interval of inversion (§ 9).   If we thus invert (*b*) we shall get this form —

Now let us compare this with (*a*).   We see that the seventh has become a third, the third a seventh, the sixth a fourth, and so on. In each case, the addition of the two intervals gives the number 10; the counterpoint is therefore in the ninth (§ 8).

222. II. *Double counterpoint in the eleventh.* This counterpoint is, on the whole, much less difficult and troublesome than that in the ninth.   The inversions are the following—

INTERVALS :   1   2   3   4   5   6   7   8   9   10   11

INVERSIONS :   11   10   9   8   7   6   5   4   3   2   1

Here, as with the ninth, there is only one consonance which does not become a dissonance when inverted ; but there is this advantage that, as the consonance in question is the sixth, we can use it more than once consecutively.   We shall see presently that in no other of these rarer counterpoints is there any interval which can be used in the same way.

223. Our first example is by Cherubini, and is taken from his "Treatise on Counterpoint and Fugue"—

CHERUBINI.

Various other transpositions are, of course, possible, *e.g.*, the subject might be transposed a fourth higher, and the counterpoint an octave lower; or the subject might be transposed a fifth lower, while the counterpoint keeps its place, &c. Notice the importance given in this example to the interval of the sixth.

224. The next illustration is taken from that exhaustless mine of counterpoint, the immortal "Forty-Eight Preludes and Fugues"—

It will be seen that the counterpoint is not strictly carried on to the end of the inversion, to which Bach has added a lower part. It is very seldom that these rare counterpoints are continued for more than a few notes.

225. The following curious, though very fragmentary, passage from Bach deserves quotation—

The first bar of (*a*) is inverted at (*b*) in the eleventh, and at (*c*) in the ninth. It should be said that there are not really consecutive fifths at (*b*), as would appear from this extract; the accompanying harmony, which we have not given, shows that the fifths are accented passing notes.

226. Our last example of this double counterpoint will be from Beethoven's Mass in D, in which marvellous work examples of all the rarer counterpoints are to be met with—

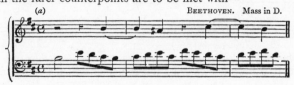

It is curious that in this example the sixth, the only consonant interval, is not used at all except as a passing note.

227. III. *Double counterpoint in the thirteenth.* The table of inversions for this counterpoint will be—

Intervals:	1	2	3	4	5	6	7	8	9	10	11	12	13
Inversions:	13	12	11	10	9	8	7	6	5	4	3	2	1

The thirteenth is a compound interval, an octave and a sixth; and it will be seen from the above table that these two intervals are the only consonances which remain consonant when inverted. Though we have here two such intervals, while in double counterpoint of the eleventh we had only one, we are in reality no better off—rather worse, in fact, because we cannot use consecutive sixths.

228. Our first specimen of this counterpoint is from Cherubini—

As with other double counterpoints, various other methods of inversion are possible. We give the commencement of two—

The student will notice that, although we call these two positions "inversions," the counterpoint is still above the subject, *but at a different interval from before.*   At (*a*) the subject is a third lower, and the counterpoint is unchanged ; but at (*b*) the subject is unchanged (except as to its octave), and the counterpoint is a sixth lower.   We have purposely chosen these positions to make clear to the student's mind a point which has more than once been incidentally touched on.   In any double counterpoint, other than that in the octave, the counterpoint is frequently seen in the same relative position to the subject, but at a different distance. In such a case, inversion, *followed by re-inversion in the octave,* is always implied.   In the present examples, if the student will invert (*a*) and (*b*) in the fifteenth, he will see that the intervals they will make with the subject will be the same as in the fully-worked example.

229. Our next illustration will further exemplify this point—

(*a*) Bars 49—51.   Bach.   "Wohltemperirtes Clavier,' Fugue 4.

(*b*) Bars 79—81.

In these two passages, the relative position of the two subjects is unchanged ; but the intervals are quite different.   To find the interval of inversion, re-invert (*b*) in the octave—

(*c*)

Now compare (*c*) with (*a*).   The eighth has become a sixth, the fifth a ninth, the third an eleventh, and so on.   The two numbers added together amount in every case to 14 ; the double counterpoint is therefore in the thirteenth.   We met with a similar case in § 221 ; but as this matter may cause the student some trouble if not properly understood, it was as well to give a second illustration.

230. In treating of free double counterpoint in the tenth, we saw (§§ 156, 157) how thirds added inside a double counterpoint in the tenth would give double counterpoint in the octave.

Similarly, if we add thirds inside a double counterpoint in the octave, we get double counterpoint in the sixth, or (which is the same thing) in the thirteenth, as in all probability the octave will really be at the distance of a fifteenth. We give a very good example of this device—

Here the treble and bass of (*b*) are the inversion in the octave of (*a*); and the student will be easily able to discover by calculation that the thirds added above the bass give the inversion, in the thirteenth with the upper part, of the preceding counterpoint.

231. Our next example is somewhat, though not precisely, similar—

Here, as in our examples to §§ 221, 229, the relative position of the parts is unchanged. The tenor of (*b*) is the same as the bass of (*a*); and thirds are added *outside* the counterpoint in the octave. But if the two lower parts are inverted with the subject, thus—

it will bring the added thirds *inside* the octave; and it will be readily seen that we have here, as in the last example, double counterpoint in the thirteenth.

232. From our last two examples it will be clear that the double counterpoint now under notice shares with that in the tenth (§ 80) the peculiarity that it can be employed against the subject in its two positions simultaneously. In both these passages the two counterpoints were below the subject; for our final illustration we give a passage in which one of the counterpoints is above, and the other below. In § 176 we quoted the subject and counter-subject of the fugue in Beethoven's Sonata in A flat, Op. 110. At the 27th bar of the same movement the following is seen—

BEETHOVEN.   Sonata, Op. 110.

Here there is not the slightest difficulty in discovering the nature of the counterpoint, as the two positions are exactly a thirteenth apart. Just as the two counterpoints of the tenth move in thirds or sixths according to their position (compare examples to §§ 156, 158), those in the thirteenth move in sixths or thirds. It must be noticed that here the upper counterpoint could not be used without the lower, because of the consecutive fourths which would result with the subject. A similar case will be seen later (§ 238).

233. IV. *Double counterpoint in the fourteenth.* The last of these rare counterpoints. Its table of inversions is—

INTERVALS:	1	2	3	4	5	6	7	8	9	10	11	12	13	14
INVERSIONS:	14	13	12	11	10	9	8	7	6	5	4	3	2	1

This counterpoint resembles that last noticed in containing two consonances (the third and fifth, with, of course, their octaves, the tenth and twelfth) which remain consonances when inverted; but, just as in double counterpoint of the thirteenth, we were unable to use consecutive sixths, we are now unable to employ consecutive thirds, as they become fifths by inversion.

234. We first give an example of this counterpoint· by Marpurg—

MARPURG.

Inversion in 14th.

Note how in this example fifths are taken by contrary motion on the accented notes, and the bad effect saved by the interposition of other notes.   As in previous cases, other methods of inversion are possible; these the student ought now to be able without difficulty to discover for himself.

235. Our next example is from Bach—

(a) Bars 49—51.   J. S. BACH.   "Wohltemperirtes Clavier," Fugue 4.

(b) Bars 92—94.

We have already quoted the passage (a) in § 229; it is curious that the same counterpoint of which we there showed the inversion in the thirteenth, should here be inverted in the fourteenth—an inversion which the student will have no difficulty in verifying.

236. The following most interesting combination,

J. S. BACH.   "Wohltemperirtes Clavier," Fugue 41.

(a) Bars 6, 7.

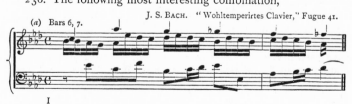

I

(*b*) Bars 22, 23.

is that which we referred to in § 221.   If the two upper parts of
(*a*) are compared, beginning at the third crotchet, with the two
lower parts of (*b*), it will be seen that they are there inverted in
the ninth.   At the same time the two lower voices of (*a*) are, as
the treble and tenor of (*b*), inverted in the fourteenth.

237. In our next example

BEETHOVEN.   Mass in D.

we have the pattern (*a*) inverted at (*b*) partly in the thirteenth and
partly in the fourteenth.   The variation arises from the modification at (*b*) of the upper part of (*a*).

238. Our last illustration is taken from the very interesting
fugue from which we have more than once quoted—

BEETHOVEN.   Sonata, Op. 110.

If the counterpoints here be compared with that of the pattern
given in § 176, it will be found that the lower voice is the inversion in the twelfth, and the middle voice that in the fourteenth,
of the original counterpoint.   Here the twelfth and fourteenth
are used in thirds, just as the octave and tenth can be.   We
assume that the student is by this time sufficiently familiar with
the necessary calculations to be able to verify the intervals of
inversion for himself.

239. If the examples and explanations given in this chapter
have been fully understood, it will easily be seen why these rarer
double counterpoints can only be used incidentally.   Whereas
in double counterpoint of the octave, tenth, and twelfth, there

are never less than four consonant intervals which remain consonant when inverted, there is only one which so remains in
double counterpoint of the ninth or eleventh, and only two in
double counterpoint of the thirteenth and fourteenth, and, except
in double counterpoint of the eleventh, no consecutive intervals
are possible.   It will nevertheless be useful practice for the
student to try to invent short passages, similar to those that we
have given in §§ 219, 220, 223, 228, and 234, which shall be in
double counterpoint with one another at these various intervals.
This will be found profitable, because complete mastery of free
part-writing is best acquired by much practice of all styles; it
will also be interesting, and even amusing, for there is no greater
delight to the earnest student than that of overcoming some
formidable difficulty.   It is for this reason that we have devoted
a whole chapter to a subject which most treatises (except
Cherubini's) either pass over in silence, or dismiss in a few
contemptuous words, as unworthy of serious attention.

CHAPTER IX.

TRIPLE AND QUADRUPLE COUNTERPOINT.

240. By Triple and Quadruple Counterpoint are meant those varieties in which three or four combined melodies are capable of being inverted in the octave, so as to be taken in any possible relative position to one another—that is to say, that each of the voices may be either an upper part, a middle part, or the bass; and in all positions the voices considered together shall form correct harmony.

241. Speaking first of triple counterpoint, it must be remarked that three parts are capable of combination with one another in six different ways. Supposing we call the three parts A, B, C, the possible combinations will be the following—

A	A	B	B	C	C
B	C	A	C	A	B
C	B	C	A	B	A

It does not necessarily follow that if we are writing in triple counterpoint, we are compelled to employ all six positions; it is, as a matter of fact, rather the exception than the rule to meet with a piece in which all six combinations are actually used; but in any correctly written counterpoint of this kind they will all be possible, and the composer will select whichever he chooses.

242. If we take the three notes of the common chord of C, and place them in their six possible relative positions to one another,

it will be seen that in two cases out of the six, the fifth of the chord must be in the bass, giving us a second inversion. For .his reason, if we attempt to write triple counterpoint in the *strict* style, we shall be unable to use the fifth of a chord at all, except as a passing note. We are thus so restricted that writing *music*, in the true sense of the term, becomes impossible under such conditions therefore, though some text-books give rules for the writing of such counterpoints, the student is not recommended to waste his time over them.

243. The simplest, but also (so to speak) the *cheapest* and least valuable kind of triple counterpoint is obtained by adding thirds above or below a double counterpoint in the octave. But a moment's thought will show the student that it is not every double counterpoint in the octave which is capable of being thus treated. If, for example, we have consecutive thirds or sixths, the additions of thirds outside these intervals will give consecutive fifths or octaves. We can, therefore, as with double counterpoint in the tenth, employ only contrary and oblique motion. But even then, we shall not always be comfortable. If, for example, our double counterpoint contains the interval of a third left by leap, and we add a third above it, we shall get a fifth, also left by leap, which in some of the positions will certainly get us into trouble.

244. An example will make this clear. Let us write a simple counterpoint of the first species against a few bars of the subject which we have so often treated in the strict style. As we are proposing to add thirds to it, to make a triple counterpoint, we will take care to use nothing but contrary motion.

This counterpoint is correct enough, though not very interesting. Now we add thirds above it—

If this is a good triple counterpoint, it must be capable of being taken in any position. Let us put the added upper part in the bass—

More atrocious counterpoint than this cannot be conceived. As we are writing in the free style, second inversions are not pro-

hibited, but they must be properly treated. Here the second
inversion in bar 2 leaps to the inversion of another chord, which
in its turn leaps to another second inversion, which is just as
badly quitted as that in the second bar.

245. It is seldom, if ever, that a triple counterpoint made by
the addition of thirds will be available in all positions. Even in
the example of this kind, given by Cherubini, in his "Treatise on
Counterpoint," we find such progressions as the following—

If we put the upper or middle voice in the bass,

we see in all examples a second inversion wrongly treated;
Cherubini, in fact, does not give these inversions. The truth is,
that this is at best a very inferior kind of triple counterpoint; the
only legitimate sort, and that which we shall treat in this chapter,
is the combination of three *independent* melodies.

246. The examples we have given in the last two sections
show us wherein the real peculiarity of triple counterpoint consists. It is in *the treatment of the fifth of the chord.* Apart from
this, it differs very little from ordinary combined counterpoint.
To paraphrase a well-known proverb, we may say, Take care of
the fifths, and the roots and thirds will take care of themselves.

247. If the student will look at the six possible positions of
a common chord given in § 242, he will see that, as there pointed
out, the fifth will in two positions be in the bass, giving a second
inversion. He has also seen in §§ 244, 245, the disastrous effect
of a careless or injudicious treatment of the fifth. What he has
now specially to attend to is, the approaching or quitting the fifth
of a chord, in whatever part, only in a manner in which the bass
of a second inversion could be approached or quitted. The
rules for the employment of second inversions are given in full in
Harmony, §§ 164, 165. Let us apply these rules to the present
case.

248. I. The fifth of a chord can only be approached *by leap* from another note of the same chord (when the harmony must remain the same, except as to its position), or from the root of the preceding chord.   If it be approached by leap from the third or fifth of the preceding chord, it is clear that when taken in the bass, the second inversion will be approached from an inversion of another chord.

249. II. If the fifth be approached by step, the preceding note may be either the root or the third (very rarely the fifth) of another chord.   It is also possible, though seldom advisable in triple counterpoint, for the fifth to have appeared as one of the notes of the preceding chord.

250. III. The fifth of any chord may not be quitted by leap, except to the root or third of the same chord, the harmony remaining unchanged.   If the fifth of a chord be either the tonic or the dominant of the key, it may remain as the root of the following chord, provided that the first of the two chords be on the stronger accent.   In all other cases it must move by step to the following note.

251. It is evident that in triple counterpoint it will be impossible to make use of consecutive chords of the sixth,

because in some of the inversions they will make consecutive fifths.   It will be well in any case to use the fifth sparingly, especially in the weaker chords of the key (II., III., and VI.): many theorists prohibit the employment of the fifth of a chord altogether, except as a prepared discord, or a passing note; but if the rules we have given be observed, it may be safely used, as no objectionable $^6_4$ chords will result from its inversion.

252. It will be advisable in writing triple counterpoint to use chiefly the strong chords of the key (I., IV., V., and VII.); and in the weaker chords it will often be well to omit the fifth altogether, as the second inversions of these chords, though not impossible, can rarely be employed with good effect.

253. It will frequently happen that some positions of a triple counterpoint will sound more satisfactory than others.   As it will be seldom necessary, or even advisable, to use all six positions, the student can select for himself those that are best; but he should at least introduce each of the three voices once in the bass.   This is the general practice of Bach.

254. It is but seldom that a composition is written in triple counterpoint throughout.   Before proceeding to give examples from the works of the great masters, we quote from Cherubini's

Treatise a short specimen, giving all the six positions, for the sake of comparison—

Concerning this very simple and intelligible example, it is only needful to remark that the fifth of a chord only appears once, at (*a*), when it leaps to the root of the same chord, according to the rule given in § 250.

255. Our first examples of triple counterpoint shall be taken from the inexhaustible Bach—

J. S. BACH.   "Wohltemperirtes Clavier," Prelude 19.

We shall give all our examples in score, that the student may more easily follow the progression of the several voices. Let the student first notice the strongly contrasted character of the three subjects. This should always be borne in mind as an important essential in writing triple counterpoint. Four of the six possible combinations are used in this prelude, and No. I. is also met with in the key of the relative minor. It will be seen that the end of the alto of No. I. is modified in II. and III.; such slight changes can always be made, if desirable, provided that they do not too far alter the character of the subject. In the middle of the theme they would be objectionable.

256. In two of the fugues in the same work (No. 4, in C sharp minor, and No. 21, in B flat), triple counterpoint is very extensively employed. The latter fugue is, with the exception of two short episodes, written in triple counterpoint throughout. Instead of quoting from these, we give a short episodical passage from another fugue in the same work, which is particularly interesting from the fact that Bach has here used all the six possible inversions. We mark the subjects with A, B, C, for their easier identification—

J. S. BACH.   "Wohltemperirtes Clavier,' Fugue 37.

It will be seen here, as in our last illustration, that the theme
which at (I.) appears in the bass is slightly altered when given to
the other voices, the rise of a fourth being substituted for the fall
of a fifth.   Observe also the way in which the fifths of the chords
are treated, and compare the rules given earlier in this chapter.

257. Our last extract from Bach is taken from the "Art of
Fugue "—

To assist the student in examining these passages, the entries of
the three subjects are marked as above, with A, B, and C, in
each inversion.   Notice here the curious changes in the harmony
produced by the chromatic alteration of notes in the subjects.
In (I.) for instance the D♯ in the upper voice is treated as the
augmented fourth of the scale, and is resolved on the first inversion of the dominant seventh.   But at (II.) the third note of the
subject C which before was a tone (G♯) above the preceding
note, is now only a semitone (D); this alters the harmony, and
here the A♯ of the middle voice is shown by its resolution on the
chord of D minor to be really B♭.   If the student will analyze
this example carefully, he will find other interesting points for
himself.

258.   In our next example

HANDEL. "Hercules."

we give only the model.   After the full illustrations and explanations already given, it will be profitable for the student to write
out the six positions for himself.   In the chorus from which the
above passage is taken Handel employs four of the six positions.

259. We next give a little-known specimen by Mozart—

MOZART. Mass in C, No. 12.

It is worth mentioning here that this extract is taken from Mozart's 12th Mass. The work usually known by this name is now universally admitted by all authorities to be spurious. The Mass here quoted was published for the first time in 1878 in the complete edition of Mozart's works. Note, as in previous examples, the contrasted character of the three themes.

260. The following example, from Cherubini's "Counterpoint and Fugue," requires no explanation—

CHERUBINI.

261. In modern compositions real triple counterpoint is very rare. The reason for this is probably to be found (at all events in some cases) not so much in the inability, or even indolence, of the composers, as in the general tendency in the direction of free part-writing which is characteristic of most recent music. For a specimen of this kind of counterpoint we give a short passage by Beethoven—

BEETHOVEN. Mass in D.

This illustration differs from those already given in the fact that the upper part is an imitation of a part of the tenor subject. In one sense it may be called an independent melody, as it differs from both the others in rhythm, having rests on the accented beats; but it has less individuality than we have seen in the examples previously quoted.

262. Our last example of triple counterpoint is taken from one of Haydn's quartetts, and is an admirable illustration of the composer's skill in combining three totally different melodies—

HAYDN.   Quartett, Op. 20, No. 6.

The small notes at the commencement are those which do not form part of the triple counterpoint.

263. If to a Triple Counterpoint a fourth voice be added which, like the others, is available in any position, we obtain *Quadruple Counterpoint.* If the student will refer to the table of positions of triple counterpoint given in § 241, he will readily see that a fourth part may be added to each of the six positions in four different ways. It may be the highest voice; it may be put between the first and second, or between the second and third; or it may be below all three. It is evident that this gives twenty-four possible positions for a quadruple counterpoint. It need hardly be added that if all were made use of, a composition would become intolerably long, and most probably extremely tedious. Composers therefore only select from this large number such as they consider advisable.

264. No new rules are necessary for writing quadruple counterpoint. As with triple, it is the fifth of a chord which needs special attention; and the student must carefully observe the directions for the management of this note given in §§ 248–250. He must also endeavour to make his additional voice distinct in character from the others. This will call his powers of invention into play.

265. Quadruple counterpoint, from its complexity is naturally

much rarer than triple, and we shall not be able to give many good examples of it. Our first will be a short specimen by Cherubini, very similar in character and themes to the triple counterpoint that we gave in § 254—

CHERUBINI.

It will be a useful exercise for the student who wishes to obtain an insight into the subject to write out all the possible positions of this little example.

266. It is very seldom that genuine quadruple counterpoint is to be found excepting in fugues ; and even in these it is more often met with incidentally than as an essential part of the structure of the piece. Such is the case in the illustrations from Bach next to be given. In the fugue in F minor, in the first book of the " Forty-Eight," is found the following passage—

(1) Bar 13.   J. S. BACH.   " Wohltemperirtes Clavier," Fugue 12.

&c.

Notice in the second and third bars, the crossing of the alto and
tenor parts.   In quadruple counterpoint, the crossing of parts is
neither infrequent nor objectionable.

267. If the above extract be examined, it will be seen that
the parts can be taken in any position.   Bach, however, only
inverts it once in its complete form—

(2) Bar 27.

Here two slight modifications are made.   At (*a*) the rests in the
pattern are filled up ; and at (*b*) the note B enters one semiquaver
earlier than before, to avoid the repercussion of the note immediately after it had been sounded in the treble.

268. Our next example is simpler in construction—

J. S. BACH. " Wohltemperirtes Clavier," Fugue 33.

Here the inversion follows immediately on the model. (Compare the example in § 256.) That the student may more readily trace the inversion, we have marked with letters the entries of the four subjects.

269. We now give two examples in which quadruple counterpoint is employed more systematically. The first is the opening of a fugue on four subjects, taken from Cherubini's "Counterpoint and Fugue "—

CHERUBINI.

&c.

It is usual for the voices to enter in succession, as here, and it is by no means necessary, either in triple or in quadruple counter-

J

point, that all should be moving together throughout.   For
illustrations of this point see the examples in §§ 258, 260, and
262.

270. For our last specimen we give a very fine example by
Haydn, taken from a fugue on four subjects which forms the
finale of his Quartett in C, Op. 20, No. 2.   As we have not yet
shown a quadruple counterpoint in its various positions, we shall
here quote the different inversions made use of in the course of
the fugue—

We see here six different positions of the four voices, out of the possible twenty-four.   To assist the student we have lettered the four themes, so that he can readily trace them in all their inversions.

271. At (I.) we have the first presentation of all the subjects together, on which immediately follows at (II.) an inversion of the same.   The slight alteration of the theme D at (*a*) is a result of the construction of the fugue, and will be explained in our next volume.   At (*b*) is a transposition of the last notes of theme B an octave lower—most likely to avoid the awkward overlapping of the parts which would otherwise have occurred.   Notice, both in the model and in the inversions, how very freely the parts cross.

272. The only point to notice in the position marked (III.) is the consecutive unisons at (*c*) between the first and second violins.   An examination of the passage that follows shows that we have not a slip of the pen here.   The first violin is beginning an ascending chromatic passage, and Haydn apparently thought the unisons better than changing the last note of the subject in the second violin.   It is perhaps such passages as this that the old composer referred to, when he said that "the rules were all his obedient humble servants!"

273. Position (IV.) is interesting as showing, not only a new disposition of the parts, but a fragmentary presentation of some of the subjects.   Only the first bar of theme A appears ; and the violoncello does not complete theme B, the conclusion of which is taken up by the viola.   Position (V.) needs no special remark. In the last position (VI.) it will be seen that the violoncello, instead of completing its theme, D, takes up at (*d*) the theme C, in imitation of the first violin, being itself imitated by that instrument in the following bar.

274. This masterly specimen of quadruple counterpoint deserves the most careful study.   One of the most striking points about it is the apparent ease and perfect fluency with which the four parts move together.   It is related of one of the old Italian contrapuntists that one of his pupils, greatly admiring a piece of very elaborate counterpoint, remarked to the master, "Ah! quanto è facile !" ("Ah! how easy it is !")   His master replied, "Ma quanto difficile è questo facile !" ("But how difficult this 'easy' is !")   Such counterpoint as that which we have treated of in this chapter can only be mastered by great patience and perseverance.   The great composers were unremitting in their studies, and any one who can write the more elaborate varieties of counterpoint with correctness and fluency may justly say, like the Roman captain of old, "With a great price obtained I this freedom."   Rules and examples will do something, but not all ; abundant practice and steady hard work are the true requisites for success.

PART II.—CANON.

CHAPTER X.

IMITATION.

275. If in a piece of music the same melodic figure occurs twice or more in succession, in the same part, either beginning each time on the same degree of the scale, or each time on a different degree, we have in the former case a *repetition*, and in the latter (if the interval of entry of each new recurrence of the figure be regular) a *sequence*. (*Harmony*, § 137.)

BEETHOVEN.   Pastoral Symphony.

In the above extract the first four bars are a repetition of the same figure; from the fourth bar to the end we have a rather free sequence.

276. If, however, the repetition of the figure, whether at the same or at a different pitch, *be in a different part of the harmony*, we get IMITATION.

BEETHOVEN.
Pastoral Symphony.

In this passage, the figure announced by the first violins is imitated by the violas and violoncellos in the lower octave; these are in turn imitated by the first violins, and these last by the seconds. It will be noticed that in the last two bars of the passage just quoted, the imitation is far from exact; it is, in fact, only a *rhythmic* imitation. This point we shall refer to presently.

277. Imitation may be either *strict* or *free*. It is said to be strict when not only the names of the intervals between the various notes are the same in the imitation as in the pattern, but when the character of the intervals is also unchanged, that is to say, when a tone is always imitated by a tone, a semitone by a semitone, and so on. In actual composition this is very rarely possible except when the interval of imitation is either the unison (or octave), the perfect fourth or the perfect fifth, above or below. A little thought will show the student that if the imitation be at any other distance, and we preserve the intervals exactly, we shall modulate—probably into some remote key.

278. Suppose, for instance, that we announce a simple phrase in C major for imitation,

and attempt to imitate it *exactly* at the second below, the imitation will be—

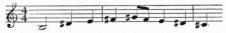

which, obviously, destroys the feeling of tonality at once. In such a case we should use free imitation, and write the latter passage without the sharps, altering the character of the intervals, but keeping the music in the key of C. At the distance of a fourth or fifth it would be possible to use strict imitation, because any modulation that might be effected would be only to one of the most nearly related keys.

279. There are many different varieties of imitation with which the student should be acquainted. By far the most frequently used is *direct* imitation, that is to say, that in which every ascending or descending interval of the pattern is answered by a corresponding ascending or descending interval, whether strict or free depending, of course, as just shown, on the distance of the imitation.

280. Imitation *by inversion* is obtained by imitating every ascending interval of the pattern by a corresponding descending interval, and every descending by the corresponding ascending. It is possible in a major key to make this kind of imitation strict as to intervals. For this purpose the following scheme is used—

The position of the semitones, it will be seen, is identical in both series of notes, and to get strict imitation by inversion it is only necessary to answer each note of the one series by the note immediately over (or under) it of the other. Thus tonic and mediant will answer each other, dominant and submediant, and so on. On this method the following passage

(A)

would be imitated thus—

(B)

where it will be seen that every interval is of precisely the same quality in the imitation as in the pattern.

281. Though this strict imitation by inversion is, as we see, quite possible, it is seldom that it is actually used by the great masters. The probable reason for this is, that (as will be observed) all the most important notes of the key—the tonic, dominant, and subdominant, are imitated by the less important ones. It is therefore far more usual, either to imitate tonic by tonic, and dominant by subdominant, or to imitate tonic by dominant, and dominant by tonic. Instead, therefore, of the imitation shown at (B) of the last section, one of the two following would mostly be employed—

282. In a minor key strict imitation by inversion is not possible. That which is to be found is constructed according to the following scheme—

If the melodic forms of the minor scale be used, the major sixth and seventh of the ascending scale will be answered respectively by the minor seventh and sixth of the descending. It will be seen that in this scheme two of the three semitones correspond in both scales, while the important interval of the augmented second, and its inversion, the diminished seventh, will be retained in the imitation—

Imitation by inversion.

It is worthy of notice that imitation by inversion is far more frequently met with in a minor key than in a major.

283. A third kind of imitation is that *with reversed accents*—
that is to say, that the notes which in the pattern are on accented
beats are in the imitation on unaccented, and *vice versa*; *e.g.*—

&c.

Here it will be seen that the lower part is a strict imitation of the
upper at the distance of a fourth below, but with all the accents
reversed. This kind of imitation is frequently called by the
name given to it by the old theorists—imitation *per arsin et thesin.*
Arsis is a Greek word, meaning "raising," and *Thesis* another
Greek word, meaning "putting down," or, as we say nowadays,
the "up-beat" and the "down-beat," in other words the unaccented and accented parts of the bar.*

284. Two other varieties of imitation are not infrequent—that
by augmentation, in which the notes of the imitation are double
the length of those of the pattern, and that *by diminution,* in
which the pattern is imitated in notes of half its length. It is
evident that more than one of these varieties can be combined;
for instance, an imitation may be by augmentation and contrary
motion, or by inversion and with reversed accents, and so on.

285. *Invertible* imitation is that which is written in double
counterpoint with its pattern, so that it can appear either above
or below it. It will be seen that the little example given in § 283
is written in double counterpoint in the octave.

286. One of the most important kinds of imitation—*canonic*—
will be dealt with in subsequent chapters; but, in addition to the
varieties already spoken of, there are two others, of little or no
practical use, which should be mentioned for the sake of completeness. These are *interrupted* and *retrograde* imitation. The
former is made by putting rests between each note of the imitation, as in the following example by Cherubini—

&c.

This is evidently a mere curiosity; and we are unable to give any
instances of its employment by the great masters.

287. *Retrograde* imitation, which is occasionally met with in
canons, is that in which the notes of the subject propounded are

---

* In old music the term *"per arsin et thesin"* is also occasionally used as
equivalent to "by contrary motion"—*i.e.,* the one part rising as the other falls.
See Hawkins's *"History of Music,"* Chapter LXVII.

given in reversed order—that is to say, the last note of the model
becomes the first note of the imitation, and so on, *e.g.*—

It is clear that contrary motion can also be combined with this
species of imitation.   It is sometimes called *imitatio cancrizans*—
"crab-like" imitation, which walks backwards, as a crab is
popularly supposed to do.

288. *Partial* imitation is when only a part, and not the
whole, of the model is imitated; the name may also be appropriately applied to such imitations as those seen in the third and
fourth bars of our example to § 276, where the intervals of the
model are not exactly reproduced, but the *rhythm* is preserved,
so that the general resemblance of the imitation to the model is
clearly maintained.

289. *Close* imitation is that in which the imitation enters (as
in the example to § 283) immediately after the commencement
of the model.   With the ordinary use of words, it would seem as
if to speak of a passage being "closely" imitated were much the
same as to speak of its being "exactly" imitated; but it is very
important for the student to notice the distinction that exists in
the technical use of these two terms.   "Exact" imitation is the
same as "strict" (§ 277), and refers to the nature of the intervals;
"close" imitation has nothing to do with the intervals, and refers
only to the distance of time at which the reply commences.

290. Though the examples we have hitherto given have
mostly been in two parts only, the student must understand that
imitation may be in *any* number of parts.   This will be seen in
the illustrative passages we shall give directly from the works of
the great masters.   Very frequently, also, imitation between some
of the voices is accompanied, like double counterpoint, by free
independent parts.

291. We now give a series of examples from the works of the
great composers, containing specimens of the various kinds of
imitation described in this chapter; it would, of course, be
superfluous to illustrate every possible variety.   We begin with an
example by Bach of imitation in the unison and octave—

The subject announced by the first violin is here imitated half a
bar later by the second, and this at the beginning of the second
bar by the third violin and the viola, all these entries being in
unison.   The final entry is in the lower octave.

292. It is not very often that a figure is thus imitated twice in
succession in the unison.   More frequently each new entry is in
a different octave, as in the following passage—

BEETHOVEN.   Quartett, Op. 18, No. 1.

Here, as in our last example, each imitation begins on the same
degree of the scale, but no two consecutive entries are in the
same octave.   In the second violin part will be noticed an
example of imitation *per arsin et thesin* (§ 283).

293. Our next example is of a different kind—

HANDEL.   "Solomon."

Here we have in the two upper parts imitation in the fourth
below; the imitation of the upper by the lower of these two
voices commences at (*a*).   The student will learn later that the
imitation here is so continuous as to make the passage into a short
canon; we have quoted it in this place as a good example of
imitation with a free bass part added (§ 290).

294. In the following passage

CHERUBINI.   "Medea."

a short figure, first announced in the bass, is imitated at various
intervals; it will be seen that with some of the entries the
imitation is only partial.

295. We next give a sequential imitation in the second above
upon a pedal bass—

HAYDN.   Symphony in G, No. 51.

296. The following extract from one of Beethoven's quartetts

BEETHOVEN.   Quartett, Op. 18, No 3.

shows imitation at various distances.   It will be seen that there is
no regularity in the intervals of entry of the different parts.

297. Our next illustration is somewhat different—

BEETHOVEN.   Sonata, Op. 10, No. 3.

Here the figure announced in the first bar is imitated in the fifth below; it is then repeated in the upper part, on which follow three successive imitations, each in the fifth below the preceding, while the last entry is at the sixth below.

298. All the examples hitherto given have been of direct imitation; we now give specimens of other varieties—

J. S. BACH.   Organ Prelude on "Ach Gott und Herr.'

This passage deserves close examination. The subject itself appears in the tenor at the commencement, accompanied by itself in diminution in the bass, first direct and then twice in an inverted form.   In the alto we have the subject first direct, and then inverted and diminished; lastly, the treble enters with the subject in augmentation. It would also be possible here to regard the treble as the original model; in this case the other parts would give us examples of diminution and double diminution.   It should be added that the frequent treatment of the phrase by inversion doubtless here results from the fact that the next notes of the melody of the choral are themselves the inversion of the first notes—

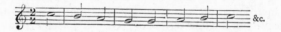

299. Our next illustration

SCHUMANN.   "Faust."

shows a simple imitation in direct motion by augmentation, and
requires no further explanation.   The middle voice is, of course,
free.

300. The following example

J. S. BACH.   "Art of Fugue," No. 6.

shows in the second bar the imitation of the subject announced
in the bass by diminution and inversion; while at the third bar
we see the subject diminished, but in its direct form.   Observe
that the imitation by contrary motion is according to the scheme
given in § 282.

301. We next show close imitation by contrary motion at half
a bar's distance—

HANDEL.   "Judas Maccabæus."

Though the imitation begins only half a bar after the model, we
have not here an example of the "*per arsin et thesin*" spoken of
above, because, in consequence of the rather slow time of the
movement, there are really two accents in the bar; thus the
second notes of the model and imitation alike come upon
accented beats, though the one is a stronger and the other a
weaker accent.

302. It was said above that imitation by inversion was rarer
in a major than in a minor key.   The following passage is an
example of the former—

MENDELSSOHN.   Overture, "Melusina."

pp   &c.

It will be seen that here the imitation is not strict as to intervals, a tone between the sixth and seventh quavers of the model being imitated by a semitone, and a semitone between the two last quavers being imitated by a tone. But the general resemblance of the two passages is much better preserved by answering tonic by dominant and dominant by tonic, as here, than would have been the case had Mendelssohn followed the scheme shown in § 280, and made the imitation strict, in which case the reply would have suggested the key of C sharp minor.

303. In the following well-known passage from the "Messiah"

HANDEL   "Messiah."

(*a*)

is seen a good example of close imitation *per arsin et thesin* in triple time, and also of *partial* imitation (§ 288). It will be seen that from (*a*) the treble ceases to imitate the tenor, though the composer, had he chosen, could have continued the strict imitation to the end of the passage.

304. In our next illustration

J. S. BACH.   "Wohltemperirtes Clavier," Fugue 46.

there is a double imitation *per arsin et thesin*. The two upper parts are imitated by contrary motion, at a distance of one minim, by the two lower.

305. The great fugue which forms the finale of Mozart's so-called "Jupiter" symphony is full of masterly specimens of close imitation. For our final example we select one short passage from this movement, giving only the string parts—

Here the imitation is so continuous in all the parts that (as we shall see in the next chapter) the passage is really a *canon.* The subject given by the first violins is imitated in the octave below, at one beat's distance (*per arsin et thesin*), by the second violins; the basses then take the theme in the twelfth (fifth) below, being imitated in the octave above by the violas; and this close imitation, at one minim's distance between all the parts, is continued not only to the end of our extract but beyond it. The whole movement deserves to be carefully studied.

306. The student who has thoroughly mastered the contents of this chapter will have a sufficient insight into the subject of which we have been treating, to begin to practise writing imitations for himself. His exercises for this purpose should be of two kinds. He should first try to invent short figures for himself, and to write phrases of from eight to sixteen bars, introducing the model in turn in the different voices, at various intervals, and by contrary motion, augmentation, diminution, &c. He will then find it extremely useful to take some of the chorals given in the *Additional Exercises to Counterpoint,* and write imitations above or below these, according to the voice in which they are placed. The way in which he should commence this is explained

in *Counterpoint*, § 475. He can either use figures of his own invention, or he can take material from the choral itself, as in the example given in § 298 of this chapter. (See also the fine example from Bach in *Counterpoint*, § 567.)

307. The study of imitation is not only a valuable preparation for that of Canon, but it is absolutely indispensable for any one who wishes to write a fugue, of which it is a most important ingredient. This will be clearly shown in the next volume of the present series. Its utility, however, by no means ends here. The examples we have given, especially those from more modern works, show its great value in imparting unity of character to a composition by means of thematic development. This point will be dealt with in a later volume of this series.

CHAPTER XI

THE ROUND.

308. Among the examples of imitation given in our last chapter were some which were continued for a considerable length. Imitation which is maintained continuously, either throughout a whole piece, or at least through an entire phrase, is said to be *canonic*; and if a composition is so written that the various parts imitate one another throughout, such a piece is called a CANON.

309. The student will remember that in Double Counterpoint at any other interval than the octave, while the names of the intervals remain the same in the inversion as in the pattern, their quality is frequently changed—minor being substituted for major, and *vice versa*. The same is found with regard to canons, as indeed was seen in the last chapter with imitation in general (§ 278).

310. Canons may be either *Finite* or *Infinite*. A finite canon is that in which the imitation is discontinued as soon as the pattern has been once repeated in each of the voices taking part in the canon. If, however, the close of the pattern is immediately followed by the repetition in the same voice of its commencement, so that the last part of the subject in the imitating voice or voices accompanies the first part of the subject in the leading voice, the canon is *infinite*. We shall meet with examples of both as we proceed.

311. As a canon is nothing more than continuous imitation, it is evident that there can be as many different varieties of canon as of imitation itself. Thus it may be strict or free as to interval, direct or inverted, augmented or diminished, or even retrograde. It is also possible to combine the different varieties; but in such cases the imitation is often so totally unlike the pattern that the

K

canon becomes one merely for the eye, and not for the ear.   For
instance, in the following example by Kirnberger,

J. P. KIRNBERGER.

a comparison of the lower voice with the upper shows that we
have here an infinite canon by augmentation and contrary
motion.   But will anybody who listens to this composition (if it
deserves the name) maintain for a moment that he can *hear* any
resemblance between the two parts ?   Music is meant for the ear,
not for the eye ; and, however ingenious these puzzles may be,
they are not music.   As this volume is meant to be practical in
its aim, we shall not waste time over the discussion of such
problems as these.   Life, at all events in the nineteenth century,
is not long enough ; and students who wish to study such
subjects must be referred to some of the old and curious treatises
on theory; our space will be far more profitably employed in
teaching what may be found actually useful in composition.

312. A canon may not only be at any interval, but at any
distance of time.   The simplest and easiest kind of canon to
compose is that which in this country is known as a *Round* ; we
shall therefore begin by showing how this is to be written.   A
Round is a canon in the unison—that is to say, that each voice
in turn begins upon the same note—which differs from other
canons in two respects.   In the first place, the parts all enter at
equal distances of time ; if the second voice commences four bars
after the first, the third will commence four bars after the second,
and so on.   With other canons there is no such restriction ; the
distances of entry may be, and very often are, irregular.   The
second distinctive characteristic of the round is, that each voice
completes a musical phrase or sentence, before the next one
enters, the phrases being usually of two, four, or eight bars'
length, though they are occasionally even longer.

313. Let us suppose, by way of illustration, that the round is
for three voices—this being one of the commonest forms.   The
whole of the music must then consist of three phrases of equal
length.   The first voice begins by singing the first phrase alone ;

having finished this, it goes on to the second phrase, while the
next voice enters with the first phrase, thus making two-part
harmony. The third voice then takes the first phrase, while
the second voice has the second, and the first voice the third.
The three-part harmony is now complete. The first voice,
having now sung the whole music, returns to the first phrase,
while the second takes the third phrase, and the third the
second. We here see why the name of "Round" is given to
this form of canon. It can be continued as long as desired;
but this should be at least until the voice that last enters has
sung the whole of the music once.

314. A diagram will help to make this clearer to the student.
Let us call the three phrases of the Canon A, B, and C, and put
the part for each voice on a separate line, placing the phrases to
be sung simultaneously under each other—

> *1st Voice* . . A, B, C, A, B, C,⎞
>
> *2nd Voice* . .   A, B, C, A, B, ⎬&c.
>
> *3rd Voice* . .   A, B, C, A,⎠

The music of a round is occasionally written out in full, as it
would be in the above scheme; but it is more usual to write out
the harmony in score, placing the phrases one above another, and
indicating at the beginning and end of the lines the order in
which they are to be sung, thus—

JOHN HILTON

The figure at the end of each line here shows which line of the
round is to be sung next. It will be seen that here the parts
cross freely; to this there is no objection in rounds, which do not
really contain upper and lower parts, as each singer is in turn
performing the highest, lowest, or middle part of the harmony.

315. There are two different ways of composing a round.
We may write the three parts simultaneously, as if we were
writing a three-part florid counterpoint; and to the student who
is sufficiently advanced to undertake the study of canon at all
this method of composition would probably present no great
difficulty. It is, however, open to the objection that he would
be very apt to think only of the three-part harmony, and to
forget that before the third voice has made its first entry, the

two-part harmony between the first and second voices must be correct, though of course not complete. For example, if he were writing a series of sixths in three parts, he would naturally arrange them thus—

This would be the usual disposition for the voices; but it will be seen that when only the two upper parts are singing together—that is to say, before the entry of the third voice—there will be a most atrocious series of fourths; it will therefore be necessary to arrange the parts in the following way—

It is mostly advisable in rounds to give the real bass of the harmony in the second, rather than in the third or fourth line.

316. A preferable method of procedure is the following. Begin by writing the first phrase of the round. In composing this it will evidently be necessary to carry in the mind at least the outline of the accompanying harmonies. It by no means follows that the phrase first written will be the highest part throughout when the piece is completed; because in a canon in the unison the parts are always allowed to cross freely. To the phrase first composed must now be added a second part, which will make a correct bass to it. It would also be possible, though less usual, to write the first phrase in such a way as that it would form a correct bass to a melody which would be subsequently written above it in the second part. A third part can then be added, filling up as far as possible the harmony of which the first and second parts necessarily give only the outline. The number of parts may sometimes be increased to four, or even more; but every additional voice above three makes the composer's task

more difficult, owing to the limited range of the harmony, and
the resulting close position of the voices.

317. It will be seen that this species of composition is in
reality a variety of free counterpoint—that is to say, it is a combination of as many different and independent melodies as there
are parts; and this leads us to impress on the student the
especial importance of giving melodic interest to each phrase of
the round. It is not sufficient that the harmony should be pure;
if this be all that is aimed at, the music will probably be as
uninteresting to sing as to listen to. Look at the excellent
example by Hilton given in § 314, and observe, with all its
simplicity the absolute individuality of each part. This is a
point which in the composition of a round should never be
overlooked.

318. We will now write a round, in order to show the student
how he is to set to work. We first compose a simple sentence
of eight bars to commence with—

The only point to notice about this melody is, that we have made
it end on the mediant, instead of on the tonic, so as to get two-
part harmony for the last note when the second voice is added,
instead of finishing on the unison.

319. Our next process is to add a second part. The principles
by which we should be guided in selecting our harmonies have
been explained in *Counterpoint*, Chapter XVI. Obviously
various harmonizings are possible; we select a simple and natural
one—

(a)

At (a) we have given the root rather than the third of the
dominant chord, because the latter would have necessitated a
rather low position for the third voice, which we intend here to
carry above the first, as will be seen directly.

320. We now add a third voice, filling up the harmony, and the round is complete—

In the first and second bars will be seen an illustration (intentionally introduced) of what was said in § 315. Had the third part been written as the second, the harmony here would have been horrible, as the student will readily see. But as the fourths below the upper part are never heard without the thirds below them, the effect is unobjectionable. It should also be remarked that passages in thirds for two parts, as here between the second and third voices, are often to be met with. Care must be taken that they are not so continuous as to destroy altogether the independent character of the two parts.

321. On examining the cadence the student will now see why C, and not E, was written for the second voice. Had the latter note been chosen, C must have been the note for the third part, and the cadence, however written, would have been less satisfactory. We will try—

The cadence at (*a*) is evidently bad, because of the hidden octaves. That at (*b*) is somewhat better, but the repetition of the note C, and the ending with the fifth of the chord at the top

can hardly be recommended.   If we alter the end of the third
voice, so as to keep it below the others,

the cadence, though not wrong, is weaker than that we have
chosen, because of the repetition of the B in the lowest part.
The melody of the third voice is also far less good than as we
have written it.

322. If we now try to add a fourth part to this already
complete piece, our difficulties will be considerably increased.
There is not much room left for a new voice.   Clearly it cannot
be either a new upper or a new lower part throughout, or it will
exceed the range of the voice.   It will have for the most part to
thread its way in and out among the others, and some care will
be required to give it an independent melody.   In many places
it must necessarily be in unison with one of the other parts.   It
is, however, by no means impossible to add such a part : here is
one way of doing it—

The compass of the voice part is here rather large, but it is not beyond that of a mezzo-soprano, and therefore allowable. Note the new character given to the third bar by the addition of a fresh bass to the harmony.

323. We shall now give a few examples of this form of canon. Our first will be a well-known specimen by Dr. Hayes—

The only point to notice in this round is that at (*a*) we see motion from the second into the unison. This is by no means uncommon in such compositions where the second (as here) is an auxiliary note; indeed, owing to the close position of the voices, it is often almost unavoidable.

324. We next give two examples by Mozart. In their published form they are printed at full length; in order to save space they are here given in the condensed form already described. The first is for four voices—

Notice in this piece the very free way in which the parts cross.
There is not one of the voices which does not, in the course of
the canon, cross with each of the others.   The pause (⌢) at the
beginning of the last bar does not here indicate, as usual, that
the notes over which it is placed are to be dwelt upon ; it is a
very common way of showing the notes on which the final close
is to be made.

325. The following example for six voices

is instructive as showing the management of a large number of
parts in a close position.   The first four bars form a kind of *canto
fermo*.   Observe the little piece of imitation in the second above
in the fifth and sixth lines. ˙

326. Our next illustration, by Beethoven, requires no remarks—

327. The round we shall next give is especially interesting as containing the germ of the favourite Allegretto of Beethoven's eighth symphony. It was composed for Maelzel, the inventor of the metronome—

328. The last example of this species of canon which we shall give is an excellent specimen by Beethoven—

BEETHOVEN.

Here we see in the second part a free imitation of the first, and in the fifth a partial imitation of the fourth. The consecutive unisons between the fifth and sixth voices are most probably an oversight.

329. Sometimes a canon of the kind now under notice is written with instrumental accompaniment of a more or less independent description. A familiar illustration of this variety is Cherubini's popular canon, " Perfida Clori," which is accompanied by arpeggios on the piano throughout. The piece being so well known and readily accessible, it will be sufficient here to refer to it.

330. We occasionally meet with a round written for mixed
voices—that is to say, as a canon *in the unison and octave.* In
such a case it will be evidently necessary that the parts shall be
written in double counterpoint in the octave. A very fine
example of this kind is to be found in the second act of
Cherubini's "Faniska"; as the opera is very little known, we
present the movement here. It has an independent orchestral
accompaniment throughout; but, to save space, we shall merely
give a figured bass, to indicate the harmonies. The canon is preceded by a symphony of eighteen bars, which it is not necessary
to quote—

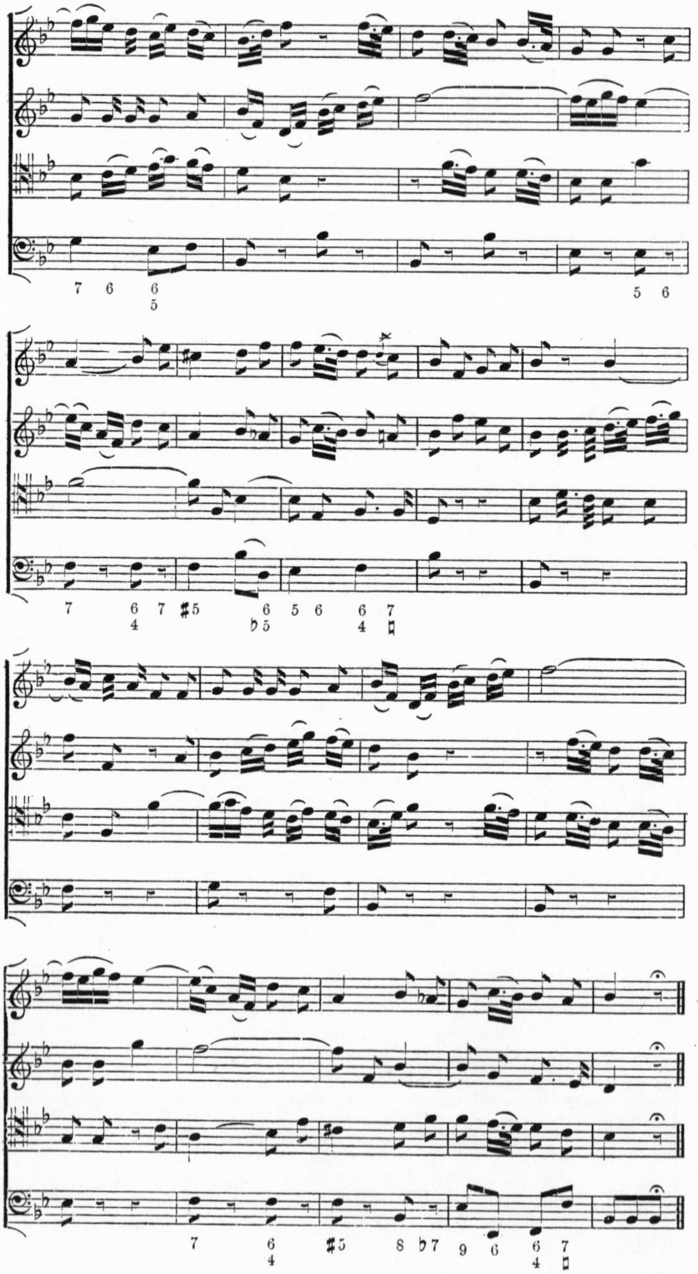

Let it be noticed that the canon is here continued until the voice that last enters (the second soprano) has sung the whole of the music (§ 313). Observe also the great increase of variety resulting from one of the parts being an octave lower than the others, the consequence being that at each repetition a different position of the harmony is obtained. The full effect of the music is also much enhanced here by the varied orchestral accompaniment, which is not given in our quotation, and which is different on each fresh entry of the theme.

331. Though it is not often that we find a complete round of the kind just given introduced in the course of a large work, there is a somewhat similar species of canon by no means uncommon, a description of which will appropriately conclude this chapter. In this form the music is carried on strictly as a canon in the unison and octave, mostly with a free orchestral accompaniment ; but the canon ceases as soon as the voice which last enters has completed the first phrase. In this form the voice that commences is the only one by which the entire canon is sung. As familiar examples of this kind of canon, may be named that in the first act of Beethoven's " Fidelio," and " Mi manca la voce " in Rossini's " Mosè in Egitto." Excellent specimens may also be found in Schubert's Masses—the "Benedictus" of the Masses in F and G, and the " Et incarnatus " of the Mass in E flat. We do not quote these, as they would only be further illustrations similar to that which we have given from Cherubini.

CHAPTER XII.

TWO-PART CANONS.

332. The canons treated of in the last chapter, though not infrequently met with as independent compositions, are seldom employed incidentally. We have now to speak of other varieties of the canon, more often used, and perhaps on the whole more useful. Though rounds are seldom written in less than three parts, other canons are very often in only two; and as these are simpler in construction, and therefore easier to compose, than those with a larger number of voices, we shall treat of them first.

333. The most important difference between the form of the canons now to be noticed and that of rounds is that in the former the imitation generally enters *at a much shorter interval of time after the pattern*—almost invariably before the close of the first phrase. The entry is for the most part about one or two bars after the commencement, and not infrequently the canon commences in the course of the first bar.

334. We said in the last chapter (§ 311) that there were many possible varieties of canon; by far the most useful is that by direct imitation; the canon by inversion is also not uncommon; but canons by augmentation and diminution are of little practical utility. We shall therefore confine our attention chiefly to the first kind, adding a few words on the others for the sake of completeness.

335. To the student who is fairly skilful in writing florid counterpoint, the composition of a *finite* canon by direct imitation offers not the slightest difficulty, whatever be the interval of imitation, or the distance of time of entry. The method of procedure is simplicity itself. All that is necessary is to write the two parts in short sections alternately. An example will make this perfectly clear.

336. Supposing that we wish to write a canon in the octave at one bar's distance. It is immaterial whether we begin with the treble or bass; in the former case the canon will be in the octave below, and in the latter in the octave above. We will commence with the bass, and, as the canon is to be at one bar's

distance, we write only the first bar in the bass, copying this an octave higher for the treble of the second bar, thus—

We next add a counterpoint in the bass to the second bar, placing it then an octave higher as the treble of the third bar—

It will be seen that all this is as easy as possible. We give a few bars of continuation for this canon, which, it is evident, could go on for a thousand bars, if desired—

337. It makes little, if any, difference in the difficulty whatever be the interval of reply; a canon in the fourth or fifth, for example, is just as easy to write as one in the octave; but there are a few points to be noticed with regard to the interval selected. It must be remembered that if the canon is at a very close interval—*e.g.*, in the unison or second—the parts are sure to cross. We saw this repeatedly in the case of the round in the last chapter. There, however, it was not objectionable, because the leading voice enunciated a complete phrase before the next part entered, and the subject could therefore be clearly distinguished. But in the canons of which we are now speaking, where the second part mostly enters very soon after the first, it will be

L

difficult, if not impossible, to distinguish the subjects if there is much crossing. A canon in the octave or ninth is therefore much more usual than one in the unison or second, and even a canon in the third would be more often written in the tenth.

338. It is also advisable in general not to make the canon too straggling, by having too long an interval of time before the entry of the imitation, because in this case the canon is much more difficult for the hearer to follow; the clear recollection of the passage which is being imitated will probably have become blurred, if not altogether effaced by the interposition of other matter. An interval of two, or at most three, bars will generally be quite enough; many of the best canons are at a bar's distance, or even less.

339. It is important to remember that a canon in any other interval than the unison or octave will be free as to intervals (§ 277); if not, the music will be in two keys at the same time. The only exception to this general rule is in the case of canons in the fourth or fifth above or below; in these it is *possible* (though by no means necessary) to use strict imitation. But it is needful to observe that if this be done we shall probably introduce transient modulations into the key of the dominant or subdominant, as the case may be; and care must be taken to restore the original key by the subsequent introduction of the necessary accidentals.

340. An example will make this clear. We will write a short piece of canon in the fourth below, *strict as to intervals—*

At (*a*) the interval of the minor third requires to be answered with the same interval at (*b*). The F♯ here evidently takes the music into the key of G. To return to the original key, it is necessary to introduce B♭ in the upper part, as at (*c*), that its imitation at (*d*) may give us F♮, restoring the key of C. Similarly, had the canon been in the fifth below, instead of the fourth, F, the subdominant of C, would have been answered by B♭; it would then have been needful to introduce a chromatic

F♯ in the upper part, that its imitation might restore B♮, the leading note of the key.   Such devices as these, though some-times practicable, are often difficult to manage, and in any case hamper the composer so much that it is usually better to write canons in the fourth or fifth free as to intervals.   It would be also possible to retain the strictness of the imitation by carefully avoiding the introduction of the leading note in the pattern of a canon in the fifth above or fourth below, and the subdominant for a canon of the fourth above or fifth below.

341. The composition of an *Infinite* canon (§ 310) is con-siderably more difficult than that of a finite one.   Till we reach the point where the leading part is about to begin the repetition of the subject, all is plain sailing; we proceed exactly as with a finite canon; but what the student will mostly find troublesome is what may be termed "making the join" neatly.   For the conclusion of the subject must be so constructed as to form a good counterpoint to what has preceded it, and also, when placed in the answering voice, it must be fitted for accompanying the first part of the subject in the leading voice.   To write such a passage sometimes requires a good deal of planning.   To illus-trate this, we will make the little canon in the octave given at (*c*) of § 336 infinite.

342. We give the last two bars of the canon as they stand. The bass is the leading part, and will therefore be the first to commence the repetition.   As we intend this to take place in the following bar, we add this bar to our quotation—

By examining this sketch, the student will see exactly what is the problem that he has to solve.   The second bar of the upper part is fixed, as also is the third bar of the lower part; and he has to invent a counterpoint which will equally well serve as a bass to the second bar and as an upper part to the third.   In the present case the task is very easy—

The double bar with the marks of the repeat shows that here the

piece recommences; but it will now be needful also to give the
sign for repetition before the second bar of the canon, thus—

Very frequently a few bars of *coda*, not in canon, are added after
the repeat in order to bring the piece to a close.

343. It will be seen that the completion of an infinite canon
in the way just described somewhat resembles the writing of a
counterpoint on two *canti fermi* at once. If, however, the canon
be at any other interval than the octave, the problem becomes
rather more complicated; for it is then necessary to invent as
the last part of the subject a counterpoint which not only fits
the preceding, but which, *when transposed at the proper interval,*
will fit the commencement of the subject. There is, unfortunately, no royal road for the attainment of this end, nor can
any definite rules be given for the purpose. It is here that the
student's contrapuntal knowledge and inventive skill will be
found most valuable, and it is precisely those who are most
at home with free counterpoint who will most easily overcome
the difficulties here to be met with.

344. We will now give a few short examples of infinite
canons at various intervals, to show the student how to write
them. We will first write a canon in the third (tenth) above —

As the imitation is here at two bars' distance, it is clear that the
canon must be composed in alternate sections of two bars each,
and not of one bar, like that which was given in § 336. The
bars forming the "join" are seen at (*a*). These had to be so
contrived as that they would also serve when transposed a tenth

higher, as a counterpoint to the subject, as at (b). Attention
will also be required to the flow of the melody; here the second
bar of (a) had to connect naturally with the C on which the
subject begins.

345. Our next canon is in the ninth above at one bar's
distance—

It is not always necessary to make the join exactly before the
commencement of the repetition; sometimes it will be more
convenient to work from both ends, and make the connection
somewhere in the middle. This was done in the present case;
it was decided to have eight bars within the repeat, so as to
form a complete musical sentence; the first five bars of the
canon were then written as they stand; the first bar of the bass
was repeated as the last bar, and a counterpoint written above
this which would make a good connection with the next bar of
the upper part. The process hitherto followed was then reversed.
The last bar of the upper part was transposed a ninth lower for
the penultimate bar of the bass; and so the canon was worked
from both ends (like the piercing of the Mont Cenis tunnel), the
actual join being made at (a). In writing an infinite canon the
join may be made wherever it is found easiest.

346. We spoke just now of having eight bars within the
repeat, for the sake of making a complete musical sentence. It
will be well for the student to try to get some kind of symmetry
and form in his canons, and not to allow them to go meander-
ing aimlessly along. At the same time, it is only right to add
that the examples we are now giving must not be judged as
compositions; they are only exercises, and have no claim to any
higher musical merit than that of correctness.

347. The following canon is in the fourth below—

It will be seen that this canon is strict as to intervals throughout.
This has been effected here by avoiding the leading note in the
upper voice (§ 340), and not, as in the canon given in the section
just referred to, by its subsequent contradiction by the minor
seventh of the key. A few bars of free close are added to this
and the following canon.

348. As the last example was strict, we will write the next, in
the fifth below, free as to intervals—

Here the tone between D and C at (*a*) is answered by the
semitone between G and F♯ at (*b*), and throughout the canon
the note C is answered by its diminished fifth below, while every
other note of the scale is answered by its perfect fifth. The
example needs no further remark.

349. A canon by inverse movement is not in general much
more difficult to write than in direct. The different methods of

inversion were shown in Chapter X., §§ 280–282. But it will
generally be found more troublesome to make a canon by
inversion *infinite*, because now the join has to be so contrived
as that its own inversion will fit the commencement of the
subject. This will often require considerable calculation as well
as much patience. Though seldom employed in actual composition, the construction of an infinite canon of this kind will
be valuable practice for the student. We give a short specimen
of this variety—

In writing this canon the join was made at (*a*) ; its inversion is
seen at (*b*).

350. It is also possible to write canons by augmentation and
diminution, and finite canons of these kinds are not at all
difficult to compose. But it will be seen that in the former, the
imitation, being in notes of double the length of those of the
subject, can only at most give the first half of it ; while a canon
in diminution must very soon come to an end, as the shorter
notes in the imitation must speedily overtake the subject. We
give two short examples—

The method to be followed in writing such canons as these is
the same as that described in § 336, except that the alternate
sections written in the two parts are not of the same length.
The asterisks in the above examples show where the canon ends.

351. The composition of an *infinite* canon by augmentation
or diminution is, on the other hand, so extremely difficult as not
to be worth the labour it requires. The special difficulty arises
from the fact that the part which is moving in shorter notes has
to be repeated against the latter half of the part which is moving
in longer notes, that is to say, against both the first and second
half of itself taken by augmentation. Those who have plenty of
time to spare, and wish to amuse themselves with problems of
this kind, will find full instructions as to how to proceed in the
large works of Marpurg and Lobe; the aim of the present
volume being purely practical, and designed to teach the
student what is likely to be useful to him, we shall content
ourselves here with giving a very neat specimen of a canon of
this kind—

It will be seen that at (*a*) the subject in the upper part recommences, as an accompaniment to the augmentation of its own

latter half. The alteration of the last bar of the subject at (*b*) is evidently necessary here to avoid consecutive octaves; but this does not detract from the merit of the canon, which Marpurg (from whose work it is taken) describes as a "real masterpiece."

352. Some further varieties of two-part canon will be noticed in the last chapter of this volume, on "Curiosities of Canon"; we shall conclude the present chapter with some illustrations from the great masters showing the use of two-part canon in actual composition. We have already, in treating of Double Counterpoint in the Tenth, given an example of a canon at that interval from Bach's "Art of Fugue" (§ 166); we now give the commencement of an infinite canon in the octave from the same work; the piece is too long to quote in its entirety—

J. S. BACH.   "Art of Fugue."

353. Our next illustration, again from Bach, is very interesting. It is a finite canon in the ninth; in the first half the bass leads, and the canon is in the ninth above; in the second the treble leads, and the canon is in the ninth below. Notice especially the smoothness of the progressions, and the beautiful flow of the melody—

J. S. BACH. " Thirty Variations.

354. A two-part canon in the unison is rather rare, though those in the octave are common enough. The following example of an infinite canon in the unison, by Mozart, is curious—

It will be seen that in the first eight bars of this canon the imitation is *per arsin et thesin*; at (*a*) a minim rest in the second voice replaces a semibreve rest in the first, thus causing the accents in the two parts to correspond for the next three bars; at (*b*) an extra minim's rest is added in the second voice, to lead back to the repetition at the original distance—three minims after the leading part.

355. In the canon just given the distinctness of the two voices is chiefly preserved by the reversal of the accents. In the following, clearness is obtained by contrast of tone colour—the subject announced by the piano being answered at a bar's distance by the strings.

The continuation of this beautiful movement contains other canons in the unison and octave, sometimes at one bar's, and sometimes at two bars' distance, and deserves to be carefully studied.

356. Our next example, from one of Haydn's quartetts, is somewhat similar in character, though presenting points of difference—

Here we have a two-part canon in the octave, at one bar's
distance, and each part doubled in the octave, as in the extract
from Schubert given in the last paragraph. But the general
effect is quite different, owing to the increased distance between
the outside parts. Notice at (*a*) the modification of the lower
part, arising from the compass of the instruments. The lower
A (the third below C sharp) would have been impracticable for
the viola and violoncello.

357. The first movement of one of Mozart's sonatas (that in
D, $\frac{6}{8}$ time) furnishes some excellent examples of canons in the
octave—

MOZART. Sonata in D.

In all these passages the canon commences with the same
theme (the first subject of the movement), though each time

with a different continuation. At (*a*) the canon is in the octave below, at one bar's distance ; at (*b*) in the octave above, at half a bar's distance ; and at (*c*) in the octave below at one quaver's distance.

358. The following example, from Dussek's sonata known as " L'Invocation," is no less remarkable for its musical beauty than for its neat workmanship—

Dussek. "L'Invocation."

The first part of this canon is in two parts only, at the seventh
below.   It is written in double counterpoint in the octave, for a
reason which will immediately appear.   At (*a*) a free middle
part is added, to fill up the harmony; and at (*b*) the opening
phrase is inverted in the fifteenth, the canon in the seventh
below thus becoming one in the ninth above.

359. Our last example is a canon by inversion, strict as to
intervals—

CLEMENTI. Gradus ad Parnassum.

M

The inversion is made according to the scheme given in § 280. The piece is very clever, but unmistakably dry, and it is given here for the sake of completeness. Whether its effect is worth the trouble involved in writing it, is at least an open question. It is extremely doubtful whether any one hearing it without any previous acquaintance would have the least idea that it was a strict canon by contrary motion!

360. The student should now try to invent canons at all intervals, after the model of those given in this chapter.

CHAPTER XIII.

CANONS WITH FREE PARTS.　ACCOMPANIED CANONS.

361. In addition to the canons treated of in the last chapter, in which the harmony is only in two parts, we frequently find compositions in more than two parts, of which two are in canon, while the others are free ; indeed, canons of this kind are probably more common than the others. It is of these that we shall now treat.

362. When we speak of the addition of a " free " part or parts to a canon, it is not meant that the added parts are to be merely a filling up of the harmony by plain chords ; the very essence of canon is contrapuntal writing ; and unless the additional parts be also in florid counterpoint there will be little unity about the composition. The new voices should be of nearly, if not quite, equal importance with the parts that are in canon ; when they are subordinate, and merely serve to complete the harmony, we have an *accompanied* canon—a somewhat different thing from a canon with free parts.

363. To anyone who is well practised in counterpoint, the canon with free parts offers little more difficulty than those already treated of—indeed it is sometimes easier, because the addition of another voice, especially when this is the bass, will allow progressions (*e.g.*, consecutive fourths) between the parts that are in canon which could not otherwise be introduced.

364. As with the added free parts to a double counterpoint dealt with in Chapter VII., those which are added to a canon may be in any position ; that is to say, the canon may be in the outer voices, in an outer and a middle, or in two middle voices. The forms most frequently met with are those in which the canon is either in the two upper, or in the two outer parts. It is impossible to give any precise rules for writing the free parts ; the method of doing this is best taught by examples, which we shall proceed to give, adding such notes upon them as may be likely to assist the student.

365. If the parts which are in canon be the two outer parts of the harmony, it is generally possible to add one or two free parts in the middle after the first sketch is completed ; but if the canon be in any other two voices, it will be necessary to write (or at least to think of) the added parts at the same time with the canon itself. To illustrate this, we will take the little infinite canon at the fourth below, given in § 347, and add a free middle part to it—

Though the new counterpoint here flows fairly well, it perhaps scarcely moves .as freely as it might have done had it been originally written at the same time with the canon.

366. If now we were to take the two parts of the canon, transpose the bass an octave higher as an alto part, and endeavour to write a new bass underneath, the music would most likely sound stiff and forced. It will be remembered that it is generally more difficult to add a new bass than a new upper or middle part (§ 195). It would therefore be better to write a new canon at the same intervals, and on the same general harmonic outline as the last.

Crossing of the parts such as is seen at (*a*), is very common in canonic writing, and quite unobjectionable. Here it was necessary in order to keep the upper part in a comfortable position. At (*b*) will be noticed what appear like consecutive sevenths. The first note, A, however, is here a passing note, and the rule is not actually broken. It is better in general to avoid even such sevenths as these, though Bach continually uses them; they are introduced here because the quaver figure as it stands gives, when it appears in the alto of the next bar, a neater counterpoint than it would have done had the bar in the treble been written

as the student will easily see for himself. It may be said in general, that in these higher branches of composition greater freedom of treatment as regards minor points is allowed than in the more elementary stages of his work. A student who has been thoroughly grounded in counterpoint will be in little danger of letting his liberty degenerate into license.

367. We will now give a canon with two free parts, and choose a rather more difficult combination than the last, making the canon in the octave between alto and bass, and adding free counterpoint for treble and tenor.　As our last canon was infinite, this shall be finite—

If the second and third bars of the alto part are compared with the corresponding passage of the bass, it will be seen that, while the notes are the same (except, of course, as to their octave), their harmonic significance is entirely changed.　In the bass the notes form parts of chords in C minor, and in the alto they are no less distinctly in E flat.　This is a frequent device in writing canon ; its employment often helps to prevent the monotony which would be likely to occur, especially with canon in the octave, from too great prevalence of the same harmonic progressions.

368. The examples we have given will, it is hoped, sufficiently show the student how to write similar ones for himself.　We now add a series of illustrations selected from the works of the great masters ; because far more can be learned from the study and analysis of good models than in any other way.

369. A most interesting work, from the canons which it contains, is Bach's " Thirty Variations for the Clavier."　Among these are to be found canons in every interval from the unison up to

the ninth, which will well repay careful examination. We quoted one of these in our last chapter (§ 353), it being the only one of the set in two parts; all the others have free parts added. We give the commencement of a few of them.

J. S. BACH. " Thirty Variations."

It will be seen that this canon is in the third below. In consequence of the closeness of the interval of imitation, we find the parts crossing here at the fourth and fifth bars, in the same way in which we have seen them cross at (*a*) in our example to § 366.

370. We next give the first eight bars of a canon in the fourth below in contrary motion—

J. S. BACH. " Thirty Variations."

This example requires no annotations ; but it may be as well for the student to compare it with the canon in contrary motion by Clementi, given in § 359, and to observe how laboured and dry Clementi's workmanship is, as compared with Bach's. Merely technical skill will never produce really artistic results in the solution of such elaborate musical problems as those we are now considering.

371. Our last example from this work is the commencement of a canon in the sixth above, which needs no explanation—

J. S. Bach.   "Thirty Variations."

372. Next to Sebastian Bach, no one has shown greater mastery of scientific resources than Mozart. We give two charming specimens by him of canons with free parts. The first is well known—the opening symphony of the "Recordare" in the "Requiem"—

Mozart.   "Requiem.

The first six bars of this passage show a canon in the second
above, at one bar's distance. At (*a*) begins a canon in the unison
at one crotchet's distance, on a pedal bass, and with a free middle
part; at (*b*) the canon is in the octave, instead of the unison.

373. Our next example by Mozart is as little known as the
extract from the "Requiem" is generally familiar. It is a remarkably neat and beautiful canon in the fifth above, by contrary
motion, and, as it is only short, no apology is required for quoting
it in its entirety—

MOZART. Canonic Adagio for 2 Corni di Bassetto and Fagotto.

374. It is impossible to draw any hard and fast line of distinction between canons with free parts and such canons as are merely accompanied. All the examples hitherto given unquestionably belong to the former class ; in our next illustration we have more of the character of an accompanied canon—

MOZART. Serenade in C minor.

Here the canon is in the octave between the outer parts, and although the middle parts are to a certain extent contrapuntal, they have none of the individuality of character which can be seen in the free parts of the examples previously given. To save space, we have arranged the passage on two staves, taking no notice of the crossing of the parts : it must not be supposed that the consecutive octaves in the fifth and seventh bars are to be found in Mozart's score.

375. The following passage is a good example of an accompanied canon—

Here the instrumental parts are strictly subordinate to the vocal, and do nothing more than fill up the harmonies.

376. Our next illustration shows an accompanied canon of a different kind—

Here the voices have a canon in the fifth below, both parts being doubled in the octave ; the orchestra not only fills up the middle parts of the harmony, but gives a florid embellishment of the canon itself. This form of accompaniment is maintained to the end of the movement, which is in canon throughout ; and in the latter half the instrumental parts become more independent, as in the following passage—

In both the above examples holding notes for the wind, which
merely fill up the harmony, are omitted for the sake of clearness.

377. Our last example will be a more modern one—

Schumann.   Albumblätter, Op. 124, No. 20.

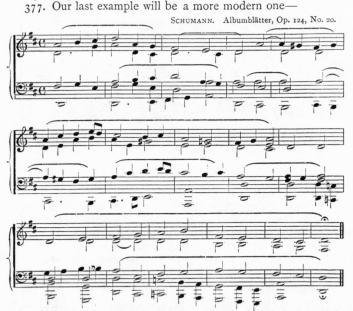

Here the canon is in the octave at one bar's distance between
the upper part, and what we should call the first tenor were the
piece for voices instead of piano. In consequence of the crossing
of the middle parts, it will require a little attention to follow the
canon in some places; it is carried on to the last note. It will
be seen that the harmony is in some places very free.

378. The student should now practise writing canons in
different intervals, and with free parts, putting the canon into
the different voices in turn. He will find this more interesting,
and little, if at all, more difficult than writing canons without
accompaniment.

CHAPTER XIV.

THE CANON ON A CANTO FERMO, OR CHORAL.

379. The last kind of two-part canon which it will be advisable to study is that in which two voices which shall be in canon are to be added to a given subject—either a simple *canto fermo*, or a choral. This is in reality a variety of florid counterpoint; but it is far more difficult than any that the student has yet attempted. He is, however, strongly recommended to devote some time to it, because it will materially lighten his labours when he comes later to deal with more elaborate canons.

380. The special difficulty of this species of composition arises from the fact that every note of the leading voice of the canon has, as soon as the imitation has begun, to be regarded from a threefold point of view. It must form a good counterpoint both to the *canto fermo* and to the phrase in the imitating voice which it accompanies; in this there is no very great difficulty; but it must also be so written that when transposed into the imitating voice it will form a good accompaniment to the following note of the *canto fermo*. It will often happen that either the interval or the distance of time of the reply will be such that it will be quite impossible to continue the canon ; in that case, a fresh attempt must be made at some other interval, or some other distance, until success rewards our efforts.

381. A short example will best illustrate what has just been said. Let us take as a subject the familiar theme—

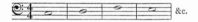

put it in the bass, and try to write above it a canon in the ninth at one bar's distance. Supposing we begin with a very simple figure—

The first note in the second bar of the alto must be one which
will not only go with the D of the subject, but which, when
transposed a ninth higher in the treble will harmonize with the
F in the third bar. A little thought will show us that B is the
only note fulfilling both these conditions; this will become C in
the treble. So far so good; but now comes the knotty point.
How can we complete the second bar in the alto in a way which
will suit, when it is transposed, for the third bar of the treble?
We cannot write thus—

because of the consecutive octaves with the bass; neither can we
take this—

for this will give us a most unpleasant mediant chord in root
position in the fourth bar. If we try—

which at first sight looks more promising, we find that when
transposed it gives us consecutive fifths with the *canto fermo*. In
fact, we are in "a tight place," and there is no really satisfactory
continuation. We therefore try again, altering the first bar, and
making the canon in the seventh, instead of the ninth, above—

The canon now goes smoothly enough.

382. It would also have been possible here to continue in the
original interval by introducing the imitation at two bars' distance,
instead of one—

383. The student will form a fair idea from the above examples of the kind of difficulty which he will meet with. In writing exercises of this kind, he should first try to work mentally the outline of a canon upon a *canto fermo*, when he has decided on the interval and distance of reply. He need not do this for the whole of the subject; but only for enough of it to make sure that he has a promising commencement; though even then he will not seldom come across a progression in the middle that stops further progress. He may find it useful in his earlier attempts to avail himself at starting of some of the models for imitation given on pages 8, 9, of the *Additional Exercises to Counterpoint.* He must also be prepared for many disappointments; at first, indeed, he will probably have at least two or three failures to every success.

384. We will now give some examples of canons in various intervals, using the same two subjects as *canti fermi* that we have so often treated for counterpoint. We first take our major subject in the bass, and write above it a canon in the seventh below—

It is only needful to remark of this, as of the other examples we shall give, that they are written in *free*, not in strict counterpoint. Thus at (*a*) we have two chords in the bar, the second (at the fourth beat) being the third inversion of the dominant seventh. The seventh is not really doubled, as the F in the alto is only a passing note. It must further be said that in all the examples we shall find a certain amount of stiffness. Under such limitations it is almost impossible to make the parts move freely. Correctness must be the first thing aimed at; but in general it would require a genius little less than Sebastian Bach's to make such exercises very interesting musically. The student must be content if he can make them fairly melodious.

N

385. We now take the subject in the treble, writing below it a canon in the fifth, again at one bar's distance—

There is no special objection here to the consecutive octaves by contrary motion between the treble and alto in the first and second bars, for two reasons.   In the first place, they are between tonic and dominant, and are, therefore, allowed occasionally in the free style; and besides this, as we are not restricted to one chord in a bar, we are fairly justified in assuming that the E at the end of the first bar represents a submediant chord.   The harmony at the entry of the tenor is, of course, the third inversion of the dominant seventh.   The close of the canon is free; this is always allowed where necessary.

386. For our last example in a major key we put the subject in the middle, and write a canon in the octave above, at two bars' distance—

This requires no explanation; it will be seen that the canon is here continued to the last note.

387. We next take our minor subject, placing it in the bass, with a canon for treble and alto in the fourth above—

Here again the canon is continued to the end. Notice at (*a*) how the consecutive fifths between the first notes of the treble and bass of the fourth and fifth bars are saved by the clear indication of a new chord at the half bar.

388. Our next canon shall be in the octave, at only half a bar's distance—

In order to preserve the canon, it has been needful here to make

the harmony in the sixth and seventh bars somewhat free.   The
harmonic framework of these bars is—

but without the addition of free parts it is impossible to make it
complete.

389. To write a canon by inverse movement upon a *canto
fermo* is even more difficult than to write one in direct movement,
and the result will in most cases not be worth the trouble
involved—that is to say, from a *musical* point of view.   Such is,
at any rate, our own opinion of the following specimen, which
has been produced with some little labour, merely to show the
possibility of a canon of this kind—

390. After working several canons on a *canto fermo*, the
student will find what we have described as "making the join"
in an infinite canon (§ 341), considerably easier; for here he has,
so to speak, to make a join in every bar.   The work is also very
interesting for its own sake; and the fluency in part-writing
acquired by its practice will well repay the learner for the hard
work that it demands.

391. There are two methods of writing a canon upon a choral.
The simpler, and easier, is to treat the choral itself as the subject
of the canon, and to add one or more free parts to it.   To do

this, it is first necessary to find a choral which will work in canon—that is to say, which can be imitated by itself at some given interval throughout. This is the chief difficulty, for it is by no means every choral which is capable of being treated in this way; but when this is once done, the addition of free parts will be fairly easy for students who have mastered the preceding chapter.

392. As an illustration, we will write a canon on the choral, "Jesu, der du meine Seele." An examination of the melody shows that it can be made to work throughout as a canon in the seventh below. At this interval the canonic voices will evidently be too near to one another for both to be treated as outside parts. We therefore take them as treble and tenor, adding free parts for alto and bass—

393. This example has several points calling for remark. Note first that, in order to give unity of character to the music, the moving figure of crotchets is maintained persistently, either in the alto or the bass, till the last bar. The canon in the tenor commences at two bars' distance; but, though it is desirable to retain the same distance of *interval* throughout a canon of this kind, there is no objection to altering the distance of *time*; indeed, this is sometimes absolutely necessary (as we shall see directly with this very choral), if we are to continue the canon at all. At (*a*) the D in the tenor is made natural for harmonic reasons; as a canon in the seventh is never strict as to interval, such chromatic alteration as this can always be made where found expedient.

394. At (*b*) the first eight bars of the melody are repeated; to avoid monotony, it is desirable, where practicable, to change the harmony. As the canon in the tenor has to be retained, we are, of course, somewhat limited in our choice of chords; but it will be seen that, notwithstanding this, considerable variety is possible.

395. The entry of the tenor at (*c*) should be particularly noticed. If the student will try, he will find that there is no other point of entry at which the canon in the seventh can be continued. Here we have three consecutive fourths with the treble. It will now be seen why we gave the imitation to the tenor and not to the bass. Had the canon here been in the outer parts, or in the alto and bass, it could have been carried no further; but the addition of the other voices here makes the harmony quite correct (§ 363).

396. In the next line of the choral it is necessary to vary the distance of time of the imitation. Had we not inserted a bar's rest in the tenor before (*d*), it is evident that we should have had consecutive fifths with the treble. Here the canon is at three

bars' distance.   At (e), by omitting in the tenor the two bars'
rest of the treble, we reduce the distance of time between the
two parts to one bar.

397. It is hoped that these explanations will sufficiently show
how a canon of this kind is to be written.   We now give a few
short examples from the organ works of Bach.   The first is the
commencement of a canon in the octave *—

J. S. BACH.   Organ Prelude on " Gottes Sohn ist Kommen.

At (a) it will be seen that the imitation of the preceding bar of
the pattern is not exact.   In consequence of the difficulty of
writing such canons as these, slight modifications of detail are
allowed, provided they do not obscure the imitation.

* In the original, the lower voice of the canon, which we have here printed on
the middle staff, is given to the Pedal, and marked " Trompete, 8 ft." As it
is the middle part of the harmony, we have altered the relative position of the
two bass lines in order to make it easier for the student to read.

398. In the example just given the canon is between treble and tenor. In the next it will be between the outside voices—

J. S. BACH.   Organ Prelude on " Erschienen ist der herrliche Tag."

The ⌒ marked here indicates, not a pause on the notes as usual, but simply the end of a line of the melody. This example is quoted to show how much freedom Bach occasionally allows himself in the treatment of a canon of this kind. Let the student compare the melody of the upper part from (*a*) with that of the bass from (*b*).

399. Our last example of this species of canon is in the fourth below, and in five parts—

J. S. BACH.   Organ Prelude on " Liebster Jesu, wir sind hier."

MANUAL.

PEDAL.

This little piece is written for two manuals and pedal, the right
hand part being marked *forte*, to bring out the canon distinctly,
and the left hand *piano*, containing merely the accompanying
counterpoints. The form of the melody is here somewhat
altered, to enable the composer to treat it in canon; the more
usual form can be seen in the *Additional Exercises to Counterpoint*,
page 12. Notice, also, the curious harmony of the cadences—
free, even for Bach, but necessitated here by the restrictions
under which he is working.

400. The second, and more difficult, way of writing a canon
upon a choral is to treat the choral itself as a *canto fermo*, and
to write upon it two parts in canon, with or without the addition
of free parts. The material of the canon may be taken from the
choral itself, but this is optional. It will generally be found convenient to commence the canon alone, and to let the choral
enter later; it is usual, also to separate the different lines of the

choral by rests, during which the canon must, of course, be continued. In a canon of this kind the choral is usually given in
long notes; this allows more frequent changes of harmony in the
canon itself, and to some small extent lightens the student's
labours.

401. The general principles by which we should be guided in
attempting a canon of this kind are the same that have been
explained in the earlier part of this chapter in connection with a
canto fermo; but the difficulty of obtaining a really artistic result
is so great that but few specimens of the kind are to be met with.
Probably the finest example in existence is Bach's Canonic
Variations for organ on Luther's Christmas Hymn, "Vom
Himmel hoch da komm' ich her." The whole piece is worthy of
careful examination; we give the opening bars of the first four
variations.

402. The first variation is a canon in the octave, at a quarter
of a bar's distance, with the choral on the pedals—

J. S. BACH. Canonic Variations on "Vom Himmel hoch da komm 'ich her.

Here the subject of the canon is quite independent of the choral,
each line of which enters, like the first, after a bar and a half's
rest. The florid canon, which, though in the octave, is not
entirely strict as to intervals, is kept up to the last note of the
variation. It ought to be mentioned that the piece is written for
two manuals; this will explain the frequent crossing of the parts
to be met with in some of the extracts.

403. In the second variation, the choral is again in the pedals,

and the canon is now in the fifth below, at half a bar's distance, the opening theme being the commencement of the choral—-

J. S. BACH.   Canonic Variations on "Vom Himmel hoch da komm 'ich her.'

404. With all their ingenuity, the two variations of which we have quoted the first bars are simple, compared with those that follow, which show what is possible in the way of scientific device to a composer with the genius of Bach. The third variation begins thus—

J. S. BACH.   Canonic Variations on "Vom Himmel hoch da komm 'ich her."

Here we have a canon in the seventh above at half a bar's distance, accompanied with a florid free part. It will be seen that the first four bars of the canon are made of sequential repetitions of the first phrase of the choral. This phrase is resumed in the last bar of our quotation, and continues to be a prominent feature in the whole variation. The choral, treated as a *canto fermo*, is here in the upper part.

405. The fourth variation is perhaps even more astonishing. It is a canon in the octave by augmentation, continued for forty two bars, with a free middle part, the choral being again on the pedals—

J. S. BACH.   Canonic Variations on " Vom Himmel hoch da komm ich her."

406. The last variation, which we only refer to here, as it is not an illustration of the species of canon we are now treating, introduces the choral in canon by contrary motion in the sixth, third, second, and ninth, and winds up with a most marvellous *tour de force,* the four lines of the choral being simultaneously introduced as counterpoints to one another! Let the student carefully examine this wonderful piece, and then go and do likewise—if he can! In any case, the study and analysis of the scientific masterpieces of Bach cannot fail to be of the greatest benefit to him.

CHAPTER XV.

CANONS ON ONE SUBJECT, IN MORE THAN TWO PARTS.

407. There is practically hardly any limit to the number of parts in which it is *possible* to write a canon; though if the number of voices be very large the composition becomes confused, owing to the continual crossing of the parts, which renders it impossible to hear the separate melodies distinctly. In a later chapter (§ 474) we shall give an example of this kind. But canons for three, four, or five voices are by no means unusual, and it is of those that we have now to speak.

408. As with the canons in two parts, treated of in preceding chapters, those in more than two parts may be at any interval. But it is most usual to write canons in three and four parts, either in the unison and octave (as we have already seen with the Rounds in Chapter XI.), or, if they are for mixed voices, to combine canon in the octave with that in the fifth. Thus, if a canon were for four voices—treble, alto, tenor, and bass—the general arrangement would be that the canon in the alto would be in the fourth or fifth below the treble, that in the tenor would be at the octave below the treble, and that in the bass an octave below the alto. This, however, is by no means obligatory, and we shall give presently examples of canons at other intervals than these.

409. No fresh directions have to be given for writing canons in more than two parts. The method of procedure is the same as before. (See § 336.) Having decided on the number of parts, their interval, and distance of entry, we write the first part down to the point where the second voice enters. We then copy the subject, as far as we have written it, into the line of the second voice, adding a counterpoint for the first voice, and continue as with a two-part canon until the entry of the third voice. We then write the commencement of the subject in the third voice, adding to it the counterpoint in the second voice which was before in the first—of course transposing to the proper interval if the canon is not in the octave or unison. In this order we continue to the end, writing the parts which are already fixed first, and adding the new counterpoints later.

410. As an example of this system of working, we will take the commencement of Byrd's universally-known canon, "Non nobis, Domine," for three voices, and show how such a piece is to be composed The number over each bar indicates the order in which it would most probably have been written down—

The canon here is led by the alto, answered a fourth below (in the dominant), by the tenor in the second bar, and an octave below by the bass in the fourth bar. We do not, of course, maintain that Byrd certainly wrote down the parts in the order which we have shown here; because a composer for the most part carries on his work to a considerable extent in his head before he commits anything to paper; but what we do point out by the figures we have given is the order in which the different voices must be added. Thus, after the first three bars were written for the alto and tenor (1 to 5), the next three bars were fixed, so far as the bass was concerned, therefore, 6, 7, and 8 would most likely be the next to be put down; 9 is also fixed, as the imitation of 5; 10 follows naturally as the accompaniment of 9; and this in its turn is transposed as 11. The student will easily follow this analysis to the end of the extract.

411. It will now be readily understood that the general principles which guide us in this kind of composition are in the main the same as those which we indicated in the last chapter, when treating of the writing of canons on a *canto fermo.* Every note added in the leading voice has to be considered, not only in its relation to all the parts which it is actually accompanying, but in its relation to those which when transposed into another voice it will have to accompany in some subsequent bar. It will also be seen how impossible it is to lay down any absolute rules for our guidance; because a rule which might apply perfectly well for a transposition at one interval, might be (and probably would be) quite useless at some different interval, or distance of time. The whole thing is a matter of practice, of calculation, and of facility in counterpoint; and it is in this respect that the working of canons on a *canto fermo* is so valuable as a preparatory step. The student will find a three or four-part canon little, if at all, more difficult than the exercises prescribed for him in the preceding chapter. All we can do now to assist him is to furnish

him with models of various styles for analysis and imitation. His own industry and perseverance must do the rest.

412. As a particularly neat specimen of an infinite three-part canon, we first give the whole of the "Non nobis," of which we have been examining the opening bars—

W. BYRD. " Non nobis, Domine.

The pause in the fourth bar indicates, as in some of our preceding examples, the place at which the music ends. As the canon is only in the octave and fourth, it is strict as to intervals (§ 277); at (*a*) the minor seventh of the scale is therefore introduced (§ 340), as otherwise, the imitation of the leading note by the tenor in the next bar would have induced a modulation into the key of the dominant.

413. Our next specimen is by Friedemann Bach—

W. FR. BACH.

Here the canon is in the fourth and octave above; in our last example we saw the fourth and octave below. Here, also, the imitation in the octave precedes that in the fourth, and the latter is not, as in Byrd's canon, strict as to interval.

414. The two following canons—both finite—are by Mozart—

In this example, in the unison and octave, it is only needful to call attention to the frequent crossing of the two upper parts (§ 337). Here the clearness of the imitation is preserved by the contrasted rhythm of the two parts which lie close together.

O

415. In our next example, the second voice enters at the distance of a second above the first, and the third at the sixth below the first—of course, the inversion of the third above—

In both this and the preceding canon the close is free.

416. It is far from easy to write a canon in more than two parts upon a *canto fermo*; the following example, taken from Cherubini's work, will show that it is not impossible—

417. It has been already said (§ 408) that in four-part canons it is very common to find the imitation at the fifth and octave. Such is the case in the first specimen of this kind to be given—

G. ALBRECHTSBERGER.

The occasional introduction of rests, as here in the sixth bar, is frequently advisable in canons, as it renders the next entry of the leading part, as also of its later imitation, more clearly perceptible to the hearer.   In the above canon the close from (*a*) is free.

418. Our next illustration is a very beautiful specimen of a four-part canon in the fifth and octave at only one crotchet's distance—

MOZART.   Mass No. 10.

Let the student compare with this the somewhat similar example of a four-part canon with close imitation from the "Jupiter" symphony, quoted in § 305.   Something analogous will also be seen in the "Amen" chorus of Handel's "Messiah."

419. Another variety, as regards interval of entry, is seen in the following—

CLEMENTI.   Gradus ad Parnassum.

The canon, which extends to 64 bars, is too long to quote in its
entirety. Though founded only on one subject, the piece has in
form some resemblance to the double canons to be spoken of in
the next chapter. The treble, which leads, is imitated by the
alto in the fifth below; the tenor and bass stand in the same
relation to one another, the tenor being a fourth below the treble,
and the bass a fourth below the alto.

420. As all the four-part canons hitherto shown have been
finite, we give next a short infinite canon in the unison—

W. Fr. Bach.

This is so clear and simple as to require no explanation.

421. Like two-part canons, those for more than two voices can be accompanied by free parts. We give an example by Mozart—

Here each voice enters a fourth higher than the preceding. (The bass enters at the fifth below, which is practically the same as the fourth above.) On the two lower staves we give the orchestral accompaniment exactly as it stands in the full score. The figured bass indicates the harmony that is to be filled up on the organ. It was not the custom in Mozart's time to write out the organ part in full, excepting where it had solo passages.

422. It was said in commencing this chapter that canons could be written in almost any number of parts. We now give

two specimens of canons for a larger number of voices. The first is by Kirnberger—

Here we have an infinite canon for six voices in the fifth and octave; the entries are alternately half a bar and a whole bar behind one another.

423. Our last example is more curious—

MARPURG.

This is an infinite canon for nine voices, the peculiarity of which is that each successive voice enters a third lower than the preceding. Such canons as these require an amount of ingenuity and patience to invent which can generally be much more profitably employed in other directions.

424. A canon is usually described according to the number of parts and the number of subjects which it contains. On the continent the general plan is to speak of a Canon "*à* 2," "*à* 3," "*à* 4," and so on; in this country a rather different nomenclature is adopted. A two-part canon, such as those given in Chapter XII., is described as a "Canon 2 in 1"—that is to say, having two voices and one subject; similarly, those we have been treating of in this chapter would be said to be canons "3 in 1," "4 in 1," and so on, according to the number of voices. If there be more than one subject, the first of the two figures shows the number of voices taking part in the canon, and the second shows the number of subjects. Thus a double canon, with four parts and two subjects, would be spoken of as a canon "4 in 2," and similarly in other cases. Canons of this kind will be spoken of in our next chapter.

425. All the canons we have given in this chapter have been written out in full, either in score, with each part on a separate staff, or in "compressed score"—*i.e.*, on two staves, as for the piano. (See examples to §§ 419, 421.) A canon written in this manner is called an "open canon." But there is another method of writing a canon, which has now to be explained. It was formerly the custom to write only the theme of the canon on one staff, indicating at the commencement the number of voices, and placing signs to show where and at what intervals the other parts entered. A canon written in this way is called a "close canon." The student must not confound this meaning of the word "close" with that which has been made use of in speaking of imitation (§ 289). As applied to canon, "close" simply means not written out in full.

426. The usual method of indicating the later entries of the parts in a canon was to place the sign § over the notes on which the parts were to enter. If the canon was in the unison, no further indication was necessary. Thus the canon by Friedemann Bach, given in § 420, would be written as a close canon, thus—

If, however, the entries of the other parts are at some other interval than the unison, it became necessary also to show at what interval these other voices entered. This was effected by adding figures to the sign §, placing the sign and figures *above*

the canon when the entry was for an upper voice, and *below* when
it was for a lower.   The figure gave the interval above or below
the first note of the subject, and did not refer to the particular note
over or under which it was written.   Two examples will make
this clear.   We will write the little canon by Mozart, in § 418, as
a close canon—

(2) à 4.

§ 8   § 12   § 5

By comparing this with the open canon, it will be seen that, as
all later entries are below the first, the figures are all under the
subject, and that they are all reckoned from D, the first note,
and not from the notes under which they are written.   Occasionally, however, this method is departed from, somewhat to the
perplexity of the student.

427.   We now give the nine-part canon of § 423 in the same
notation—

à 9.

§ 3   § 5   § 7   § 9   § 11   § 13   § 15   § 17

After what has been said, this example will be quite intelligible.

428   There is another method of indicating in a close canon
the number of voices and the order of entry.   This is, to prefix
to the canon the various clefs of the different voice parts.   Unfortunately, no uniform system is adopted as to the order in
which these clefs shall stand.   Albrechtsberger says that "when
a canon is answered on the fifth or octave above, or on the fifth
or octave below, it is usual to place the clefs of the voices, in
the order in which they are to succeed, before the clef used for
the commencement of the canon and before the signature is
marked ; then either the sign § or a figure indicating the distance
of the interval shows the note on which the successive voices are
to enter."   On this method, the notation of the canon in § 417
would be—

Sometimes, however, the clefs are all put in reversed order ; *e.g.*,
for the same canon—

while Marpurg, in some of his examples, gives the clefs in the
regular order of entry of the voices.   As close canons are seldom

written now, the matter is not of much practical importance; but it is well that the student should understand these signs if he meets with them in old music.

429. We will conclude this chapter with a specimen of a twelve-part infinite canon in the unison, taken from Marpurg. We shall give it as a close canon only; it will be interesting for the student to put it into open score for himself. He will find that the harmony is extremely simple, consisting of nothing but alternations of tonic and dominant chords—

CHAPTER XVI.

CANONS WITH MORE THAN ONE SUBJECT.

430. Hitherto we have treated exclusively of canons which have had only one subject; but it is quite possible to work two, three, or even more voices simultaneously in canon. It will be evident that the number of parts in the harmony must be at least double the number of the subjects to be treated canonically. On the continent a canon with two subjects is usually described as a Double Canon, one with three as a Triple Canon, and so on; but in England it is more usual to speak of them after the method explained in the last chapter (§ 424); and this method will, therefore, be that which we shall now follow.

431. The canons to be described in this chapter are the most elaborate, and in many cases the most difficult, that it will be necessary to study. It is true that there are other varieties which are more complicated; but these are of so little practical use that we do not recommend the student to trouble himself over them at all. We shall speak of them in our final chapter on "The Curiosities of Canon." Such double and triple canons as we are now about to notice are, on the other hand, of real artistic value; and it will be well worth the student's while to spend some time in trying to write them.

432. It is impossible to give any exact rules for the composition of a double or triple canon. Like the various kinds with which we are already acquainted, it must be worked in small sections, the length of which must depend on the distance of the time of entry of the different voices, and those parts which are fixed (that is to say, which are the canonic imitations of the themes given by the leading voices) must always be written in the imitating voices before the counterpoint is added to them in the other parts. Beyond these general directions it is not easy to assist the student, who will learn best how to work by the careful examination and analysis of the examples we are about to give him, which we shall accompany by such remarks as may be likely to be helpful.

433. We shall commence with a number of canons 4 in 2, that is to say, canons with two subjects, each subject being imitated in one other voice, thus making four parts in all. The

least difficult canon of this kind is one which resembles a Round
(Chapter XI.), inasmuch as the two leading voices complete an
entire phrase before the following voices enter.   In this case the
imitations will be almost always in the octave—either above or
below, according to the voices which are selected to lead.
Canons of this description are not very common; the following
is a very good specimen by Mendelssohn—

MENDELSSOHN.   "Lerchengesang," Op. 48, No. 4.

It will be seen that the above is an infinite canon; it concludes
with seven bars of free *coda*, which it is not needful here to quote.
As with a round for mixed voices (§ 330), it is of course necessary
that the parts should be written in double counterpoint in the
octave.

434. Our next example is taken from the organ works of
Bach—

J. S. BACH.   Organ Prelude on " In dulci jubilo.'

As in the canon from Bach that we quoted in § 397, we have re-arranged the score, to make it easier to read. The choral printed on the middle staff is in the original given to the pedals. We have here the commencement of a finite canon, 4 in 2, in the octave; it is curious that Bach has throughout the movement written triplet quavers instead of crotchets in the counterpoint. For the slight alteration of the melody at (*a*) compare § 398.

435. In the two canons last given, the two upper voices have been imitated in the lower octave by the two lower ones. In our next examples other methods of procedure will be shown—

In this very neat infinite canon, 4 in 2, the subject announced by
the alto is imitated in the fourth above by the treble, while the
other subject, given to the tenor, is imitated in the fifth below
by the bass.

436. Another specimen of an infinite canon, 4 in 2, of a rather
different kind will be seen in the following—

SCHUMANN. "Die Capelle," Op. 69, No. 6.

This little piece is the last of a collection of part-songs for female voices.   The two subjects of the canon are announced in the first bar by the two treble voices, and imitated in the following bar in the fourth below by the two altos.   Owing to the close position of the harmony, arising from the use of female voices only, it will be seen that the parts cross very freely.   The canon, it should be observed, is not strict as to interval.   There is a free *coda*, which we have quoted here, as, though not strictly in canon, it contains a good deal of free canonic imitation.

437. In § 374 we gave the commencement of the Minuet from Mozart's Serenade in C minor for wind instruments, as an example of an accompanied canon.   The trio following this

P

Minuet is a very beautiful example of a canon 4 in 2 by inversion, which is worth quoting in its entirety—

Here the second oboe is imitated in contrary motion by the first, and the first bassoon (with a different theme) in contrary motion by the second. In the first half of this piece, the variety of the imitation is that shown at (D) in § 281. But in the second half, while the oboes still retain the same imitation (answering tonic by dominant, and dominant by tonic), the second bassoon imitates the first after a different manner, answering tonic by tonic, and dominant by subdominant. (Compare (C) in § 281.) The last two bars before each double bar are free. The whole movement is a very fine illustration of the way in which, in the hands of such a master as Mozart, the most elaborate scientific contrivances can be employed without producing the least stiffness of effect; the music flows as naturally as if it were nothing but simple four-part counterpoint.

438. Our last example of a 4 in 2 canon is taken from Bach—

Here we have a canon in the fourth below between the alto and tenor, and a second canon in the fifth above between the violin and the *oboe da caccia*,* the first note of the violin part being free. The difference between this and the examples previously given is that here, in addition to the double canon, we have an independent free bass part.

439. We now give some examples of canons in more than four parts. Our first is a very charming little specimen of an incidental canon, 6 in 3, from one of Mozart's little-known Masses—

Here we see three canons, each in two parts, proceeding simultaneously; an interesting point to notice is that each of the

* The *oboe da caccia*, frequently used by Bach, was a now obsolete species of oboe, the compass of which was the same as that of the modern *cor anglais.*

canons is at a different interval.   That between the treble and
alto is in the fifth below; between the tenor and bass it is in the
seventh below; while the canon between the instrumental bass
and the first violin is in the sixth above.

440. Our next illustration is the beginning of a canon 6 in 2
in the octave from a sextett for strings by Raff—

J. RAFF.   Sextett, Op. 178.

The canon, which continues strict for 27 bars, is too long to
quote entire.   It will be seen that the harmony is at times somewhat free.   It must be remembered that in pieces of such
elaborate and artificial construction as a canon of this kind
greater liberty will always be allowed than under ordinary circumstances.   At the same time, such liberty must never degenerate
into license.

441. The following short extract from the "Rex tremendae"
of Mozart's "Requiem," is a fine example of a quadruple canon—
8 in 4—

Here there is a canon for the treble and alto in the fourth above, another for the tenor and bass in the fifth below; while the two lower string parts in thirds are imitated by the two upper parts, also in thirds, there being altogether eight parts, all moving in canon.

442. A different kind of canon (also 8 in 4) will be seen in our next illustration, which is taken from Cherubini's magnificent "Credo" for a double choir—

We give only the beginning of the canon, which extends over 38 bars, during the whole of which the first choir is imitated note for

note by the second at two bars' distance. The latter part of the
canon, which we have not room to quote, is even more elaborate
and intricate than the first. Every student should make the
acquaintance of the masterly work from which this extract is
taken.

443. Our last example is the most complex we shall have to
give. It is a short infinite canon, 12 in 4, for three choirs, and,
like the other examples by Mozart which we have quoted, is
remarkable for the ease with which the master moves, in spite of
his self-imposed fetters—

444. It will be readily seen that the composition of such canons as we have been treating in this chapter is a task of no ordinary difficulty, the more so because of the impossibility of laying down any definite rules as to their construction. More can be learned by the examination of good models than in any other way; and it is for that reason that such numerous and lengthy examples have been given. But to succeed in this department of work, not only considerable natural aptitude is

requisite, but a very large amount of practice. This will be found most beneficial, not only (nor perhaps even chiefly) for its own sake, but for the freedom of imitative contrapuntal writing which it will give. It is quite possible that a student may never want to write a 4 in 2 canon as long as he lives; but the *ability* to do so, if necessary, would be invaluable to him in such a department of composition as the thematic developments of a symphony or quartett. Besides this, the more thoroughly a composer is equipped at all points for his work, the greater his chance of producing something which is likely to live.

445. With this chapter we complete our instructions on the subject of canon. There are other varieties which we have not yet touched upon; but these are of so little practical use to the student that it will not be worth his while to waste time in writing them. We speak of them, giving examples of some of the more curious varieties, in our next chapter.

CHAPTER XVII.

CURIOSITIES OF CANON.

446. The old theorists exercised an enormous amount of ingenuity in the invention of canonic devices, many of which were of not the slightest practical use. We have already given one specimen of this kind in the canon by augmentation and contrary movement quoted from Kirnberger in § 311; and we shall now briefly describe some of the chief varieties to be met with, though, because of their mostly unpractical character, we shall not give directions as to the method of writing them. Those who are curious in such matters will find instructions on the subject in the works of Marpurg and Lobe.

447. A favourite device of these old writers was to compose a canon with double, and even triple augmentation, such as the following—

S. SECHTER.

Here the second treble shows the augmentation, the alto the double, and the bass the triple augmentation of the subject given to the upper part. This is merely a canon to the eye, and not to the ear; it is of no musical value, and utterly useless except as an exercise of ingenuity.

448. Our next example is even more elaborate—

J. P. KIRNBERGER.

&c.

Here again the subject is given in notes of four different lengths; but the alto and the first treble are in contrary movement to the other parts.

449. A species of canon frequently to be met with is a RETROGRADE CANON (*Canon Cancrizans*). In this, as explained in § 287, the notes of the subject are given in reversed order—that is, the answer of the canon is the subject read from right to left, instead of in the usual manner from left to right. Many very ingenious specimens of this kind of canon exist. The following is from Bach's "Musikalisches Opfer"—

J. S. BACH.   "Musikalisches Opfer."

(a)

If this piece be examined, it will be seen that the lower part
read backwards from the last bar to the first is the same as the
upper line read in the ordinary way.   In a canon of this description it is usual for the two voices to commence together, as in
the present example.   The upper part from (*a*) to the end is the
same as the lower part read backwards from this point to the
beginning, and *vice versâ*.

450. Our next example, quoted from Hawkins' "History of
Music," is much more complex—

W. Byrd.

Q

CANON.

We have here a most elaborate retrograde canon, 8 in 4. The second treble part is the first treble read backwards, and the second alto, tenor, and bass parts are also their respective firsts by retrograde movement. Though rather long, it has been needful to give the whole piece here to render it intelligible. Let the student notice that in addition to the retrograde imitation we have spoken of there is also almost continuous close direct imitation between the voices. Truly the old masters of the Elizabethan age possessed rare skill in contrapuntal writing!

451. Another even more intricate kind of canon is the REVERSE RETROGRADE CANON. This is a canon so constructed that when the book is reversed (that is to say, when it is turned upside down), the music shall read the same as in the usual position. This is, of course, a mere curiosity; but a few examples will be worth giving. The first is by Lobe—

J. C. LOBE.

To indicate a canon of this kind, the inverted signature is placed at the end, as here.

452. Our next example is by a living German musician, and was published in the *Musikalisches Wochenblatt—*

OSCAR BOLCK.

453. We now give a specimen by a living English composer
of a reverse retrograde canon in four parts—

F. CORDER.

F. CORDER.

This is a different kind of canon from those given above. Here there is no canon by direct motion; but it will be seen that when the book is turned upside down the whole composition is exactly the same as before. The accidentals are here printed under or over the notes, instead of before them in the usual way, as they are only wanted in one of the two positions.

454. Another highly ingenious, but, owing to its great difficulty, very rarely-used device is that known as canonic imitation *by Inverse Contrary movement*. This is a canon for a double choir, in which a theme is announced by one choir and answered by the other in the following manner—the movement is *inverse*—that is to say, the voices of the one choir are imitated by the other in reversed order, the treble of the first choir by the bass of the second, the alto by the tenor, the tenor by the alto, and the bass by the treble. Besides this, all the subjects are imitated by contrary movement. The chief rule to be observed in writing imitation of this kind is that none of the lower voices must ever sound the fourth below the treble except as a passing note. In Bach's "Art of Fugue" will be found a whole fugue (No. 12) which is inverted in this way; but probably the finest example of imitation of this kind for two choirs is in Cherubini's "Credo" for a double choir, from which we quoted a passage in our last chapter (§ 442). This great work contains a canon of this kind 77 bars in length, which begins thus—

It will be seen that the first choir commences the imitation on the
last note of each phrase sung by the second choir, and that the
imitation is carried out in the manner just described.   Towards
the end of the canon the imitation becomes closer and more
elaborate.   We give the last nineteen bars—

Here we not only have the inverse contrary imitation carried on
as before, but also direct imitation between the different voices of
the same choir. Besides this, the second choir is not now silent
when the first enters. The whole passage is a masterpiece of
scientific contrivance.

455. A CIRCULAR CANON is one which modulates so that each repetition is in a different key.* The most common variety is that in which each repetition is a tone higher than before; hence the old name for this species of canon, "Canon *per tonos.*" Obviously after six repetitions, each a tone higher, we shall return to the original key. If it is desired to pass through all twelve keys, each repetition must be either a semitone, or else a fourth or fifth, higher than the preceding. The following is a good example of a circular canon—

J. S. BACH. "Musikalisches Opfer."

* Some writers use the word "circular" as equivalent to "infinite"; but it is more usual, and also preferable, to employ it in the sense we are now explaining.

Here the upper part is a variation of the theme seen in our example to § 449. Below this theme are two parts in canon in the fifth. The music, beginning in C minor, modulates to D minor. The signs 𝕊, indicating an infinite canon, show where the repetition commences; but this repetition will now be a tone higher in all the parts. Evidently the two following repetitions will begin in E minor and F sharp minor; and so on to the end.

456. A POLYMORPHOUS CANON is one in which the same subject is capable of being worked in many different ways. The old theorists devoted much time and labour to the invention of such things. Marpurg gives the subject of a canon by Valentini which the composer worked in 2,000 different ways! But the most celebrated and best-known example of this kind of canon is one by Stölzel, written by him to disprove the assertion of an opponent that the possibilities of canon were exhausted. We give an abstract of Marpurg's analysis of this canon, which will show its chief features.

457. We first give the canon (which is an infinite canon 4 in 1, in the fifth and octave) in its original form—

Marpurg remarks of this canon that it is so constructed that we can begin with any one of the seven bars of which the subject consists, or at any half bar. For example, if we commence at the fourth bar, the subject takes this form—

This evidently gives us fourteen forms of the subject. To save space, we give this and the following examples as close canons (§§ 425–427). As the notation of a close canon has been fully explained, the student will easily be able to write them out as open canons for himself.

458. But further, each of these seven subjects can be equally well treated *per arsin et thesin*. We give the original form thus altered as a specimen of them all—

This clearly gives fourteen canons more, making twenty-eight.

459. The next step is to treat the subject by inverse contrary movement, as in the example by Cherubini in § 454. The canon then assumes the following form—

Pursuing the same method as before—that is, beginning at any half bar, and also treating the various forms of the subject *per arsin et thesin*, we obtain twenty-eight new canons, making altogether fifty-six.

460. The subject in the form first shown can also be taken by retrograde motion, altering the time values, where necessary, and introducing passing notes, to obtain a better melody. This produces the following—

which can be varied in the same way as those preceding. This last given theme can also be inverted—

461. By beginning with one of the middle voices, and varying the distance of time of entry, and the order of entry of the voices, many new combinations are obtained—

The total possible combinations already given amount, according to Marpurg, to 392.

462. A new series of canons is obtained if we make the imitation closer. It will suffice to give one as an example—

Eighty-four combinations of this kind are possible.

463. Lastly, the canon can be treated as a circular canon, by recommencing on the fourth below and fifth above alternately at each new repetition.   The following example will show this clearly.   The * shows the note on which in each of the voices the subject begins afresh—

Evidently we shall go through the entire "circle of fifths," and ultimately return to the key of C.

464. It need scarcely be said that but few subjects are capable of such infinite variety of treatment as that which has just been shown ; but it is by no means difficult to write short and simple subjects for canon which are capable of many different treatments ; and although a polymorphous canon is of but little use for its own sake, the practice of writing such is very valuable as a preliminary study for the *stretto* of fugues, as will be explained in the next volume of this series. To afford the student an opportunity of exercising his ingenuity in this direction, we give the subject of a polymorphous canon from Marpurg—

This simple scale passage can be treated as a canon at any interval, above or below, either by direct, contrary, or retrograde motion, *per arsin et thesin*, and by augmentation and diminution. Marpurg shows that more than a hundred different canons are possible on this subject in two parts only, while by adding thirds, sixths, or tenths to either or both of the two parts, the number of possible combinations is increased to over a thousand. And all this can be done with a simple scale !

465. The last kind of canon we shall describe is the RIDDLE-CANON. This is a variety of close canon (§ 425), in which the usual signs to indicate the place and interval of entry of the different voices are omitted. The number of voices is mostly given, though sometimes not even this is done. The old theorists wasted an immense amount of time and ingenuity in the invention and solution of such puzzles as these, with regard to which Marpurg pithily remarks that one fool can ask questions

which ten wise men cannot answer. We give a few curiosities of
this kind; the first is from Martini's "Storia della Musica"—

Plutonica subiit regna.
(*a*) Canon ad Diapason-Diapente.   MARTINI. "Storia della Musica."

Tertia pars, si placet.

Here more clue to the solution is given than in some cases.
The "Diapason-Diapente" is the Greek name for the interval of
the twelfth; and the Latin motto, "Plutonica subiit regna" ("He
went down to the realms of Pluto"), is an obscure method of
hinting that the canon must begin by *descending*. Here, therefore, is to be a canon in the twelfth by contrary motion, and the
puzzle is to find where the imitation is to commence. The
"tertia pars, si placet"—the third part, if desired—indicates a free
bass *ad libitum*. The canon, it will be seen, is infinite, and the
solution * is the following—

Of course the treble does not enter at first until the fourth bar.

466. A considerably more difficult example of a riddle-canon,
taken from the same work, is the following—

* Reprinted by permission from the *Musikalisches Wochenblatt.*

MARTINI. "Storia della Musica."

Here we see that there are two subjects, before each of which four clefs are placed ; each is therefore to be sung by four voices, and the canon will be 8 in 2.   The direct (w) put at the end of each subject, and referring back to the first note, shows that the canon is to be infinite.   But no clue is given as to the order, interval, or distance of time of entry of the different voices.   To solve such a riddle-canon as this, it would be needful to try the subjects at all possible intervals, by direct, inverse, and retrograde imitation, even by augmentation and diminution, until success rewarded our efforts.   In the present case the true solution was given in the *Musikalisches Wochenblatt* for 1880.   We reprint it, as a remarkably neat specimen—

Each subject is here treated as a canon in the fifth above, the second choir entering four bars after the first.

467. Two very clever riddle-canons, one for two, and the other for four voices, are to be found in Bach's "Musikalisches Opfer." The former, to which the composer has prefixed the motto "Quærendo invenietis" ("Seek, and ye shall find"), is capable of four different solutions. Both canons are unfortunately too long to quote here.

468. That the art of composing riddle-canons is not yet lost will appear from the following very ingenious example by Fr. Link, which was published some years since in the *Musikalisches Wochenblatt*—

DUO FOR TWO VIOLINS.

Allegretto.　　　　　　　　　　　　　　　　　　　Fr. Link.

This veritable puzzle illustrates a variety of riddle-canon which we have not yet seen—that in which the bars are not to be read in the usual order; it is somewhat similar to the *canon cancrizans* (§ 449), though with a difference. The difficulty is to discover

the order in which the bars are to be taken.   The only clue
afforded is the double bar in the third line, which seems to
suggest that this is the final bar of the piece.

469. The author's solution of the riddle is as follows: "The
above piece in two parts is a special modification of the retrograde canon by contrary motion (*canon cancrizans in motu
contrario*).   The first part begins above at the first bar, and takes
all the bars in the order indicated by the figures—

when the notes of bars 9, 10, 11, 12, 13, 21, 22, and 23, must be
read *backwards*—from right to left.   The close of this part is bar
25 in the middle.   The second part turns the music upside
down, as shown by the clefs, and performs the whole piece
simultaneously with the first part, beginning with bar 25 of the
first part.   The second part takes the bars in the order indicated
above them, reading the notes of bars 3, 4, 5, 13, 14, 15, 16, and
17 backwards—from right to left.   This part ends with bar 1 of
the first part, which is its 25th bar.   The succession of the bars
is arranged as a spiral, which with the first voice runs from the
outside to the centre, and with the second in the reverse
direction; the whole in its peculiar arrangement thus forming a
so-called musical labyrinth."

R

470. We now give the two voices together in score—

It will be seen that we have here a reverse retrograde canon
(§ 451). It is of little musical value except as a curiosity. Perhaps even more surprising than the ingenuity displayed in its
invention is the fact that it should have been solved. The

solution was sent to the *Musikalisches Wochenblatt* by Herr F.
Böhme, of Leipzig.

471. The above examples will sufficiently illustrate the nature
of the riddle-canon ; we shall now in conclusion give a few mis-
cellaneous curiosities, which can hardly be classified under any
of the divisions we have spoken of.   Our first is a fine specimen
by Byrd—

W. BYRD.

Here is seen an unusual kind of 4 in 2 canon upon a plain chant
(or *canto fermo*). The chant, which is seen in the second treble
part, is the melody of the old hymn, " O Lux beata Trinitas," on
which Byrd wrote many canons. Between the third treble and
first alto is a canon in the fifth below *per arsin et thesin*; while
between the second alto and the bass is a canon in the octave by
irregular augmentation, some of the bass notes being four times
the length of the alto, others only double the length, while two
notes of the alto (the first and third minims of the third bar) are
only of the same length in the bass. The pauses in the third

treble and second alto parts do not indicate a rest on those notes, but merely show how far the canon is carried in the imitating voices. The first treble part is free.

472. Our next example, a "Miserere" by Tallis, is of an extremely complicated description—

T. TALLIS.

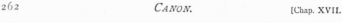

Here we have a canon 6 in 2, with one free part. Usually in a
6 in 2 canon each of the two subjects is in three of the parts.
(See the example by Raff in § 440.) Here, however, the first
subject is only given to the two trebles, which have a canon in
the unison at two minims' distance. The other subject, which is
seen in the first tenor, appears in direct motion, and in double
augmentation, in the second tenor; the first bass (which in the

original is written in the very rare C clef on the fifth line, ⧉)

is the free part; the second bass gives the subject of the first
tenor in contrary motion, and by triple augmentation, while the
third bass takes the same subject in simple augmentation, and
also by contrary motion. The amount of labour required for
writing such a canon as this can hardly be conceived. The part-
writing is necessarily somewhat free. The whole piece deserves
careful examination and analysis.

473. Our next curiosity is by Bach. It is an infinite canon,
7 in 1 in the unison, on a ground bass (*basso ostinato*), that is,
one figure continually repeated. The subject is given by Bach as
a close canon thus—

The ground bass, which serves as a perpetual accompaniment, is the following—

We give the canon in score—

J. S. BACH.

Ground Bass.

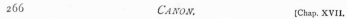

474. It was a favourite amusement with the old theorists to
practise writing canons for an enormous number of parts.
Marpurg gives the subject of a canon which Valentini wrote for
96 voices, arranged in 24 choirs, and he tells us that Kircher
discovered that the same canon could be performed by 512
voices, or 128 choirs. The subject itself consists of nothing but
the notes of the common chord. Evidently such a canon as this
has no claim to be considered as real music ; in performance
one would hear nothing whatever but the common chord, with
the parts incessantly crossing, so that there could be no clear
effect. As a specimen of the kind of ingenuity that was ex-
pended over these curiosities, we give as our last example a
canon 36 in 1, for nine choirs, by Michielli Romano, a composer
who lived at Venice about the beginning of the seventeenth
century. As it is impossible to get a score of 36 staves on our
page, we give each of the nine choirs in "short score"—

MICH. ROMANO.
1st Choir.
2nd Choir.
3rd Choir.
4th Choir.
5th Choir.
6th Choir.
7th Choir.
8th Choir.
9th Choir.

Here the tenor part of the first choir imitates the bass, by contrary motion throughout; the alto and treble commence at the half bar, taking the octave above the bass and tenor parts. Each successive choir enters in the same way one bar later than the preceding. The marks ⤬ indicate the crossing of the voices. It will be seen that the musical effect of the whole is by no means exhilarating; such canons as these are not of the slightest use when they are written. We have inserted this one simply as a curiosity, and to show the student what these canons with a multitude of parts were really like.

475. Here our task ends. The student who desires to go deeper into these curiosities can find further details in the works of Marpurg and Lobe. Our object is simply to teach such matters in connection with canon as are likely to be practically serviceable. The great use of canonic writing is not so much for its own sake as for the freedom that the study gives in fugal, and to a considerable extent also in symphonic, composition. Those who have thoroughly mastered the contents of this volume will find their acquired knowledge invaluable if they proceed to the next step in composition—the writing of fugue, which will form the subject of our next volume.

THE END.

S